How To Promote

Market And Sell

Your Kindle Book

Amazon Kindle Publishing Marketing and Promotion Guide

By Omar Johnson

Table of Contents

Introduction

This is The Only Cutting Edge Book On The Subject of Kindle Book Marketing, Promotion And Selling That Teaches You:

- How To Understand And Master The Amazon Kindle Book Ecosystem.
- How To "Scale" Your Kindle Book So That You Can Make A Lot More Sales and Money.
- How To Effectively Use The Internet and Social Media To Promote Your Kindle Book And Brand Yourself As An Author.

If you picked up this book, then there is a good chance that you're a writer or a newly published Kindle author. If you've already taken the step to publish your work in the Kindle store, you are part of an exciting new revolutionary movement within the publishing industry.

No longer do you have to worry about being rejected by the traditional publishers hoping and praying that your manuscript is the one in a million that escapes the slush pile. The days of being rejected by publisher after publisher are finally drawing to a much need close.

But of course there are some catches, like with most things. You don't have a big name publisher to market your eBooks, that's for sure. You may not even have a publicist to help you out with promotion either, as they are quite expensive to hire on.

The great thing about going the indie route is that while there may be more work involved, it's usually worth having the creative freedom and total control when it comes to your writing and what you decide to do with it.

Most newly published authors face the same challenge. They think of themselves as writers, not salespeople. They convince themselves that these two skills can't exist in harmony and they talk themselves into believing that they can't tackle their marketing and promotion on their own.

The truth is, that's nonsense.

Marketing and promoting is not the same thing as selling, per se. There is no good reason that a writer or author can't effectively market and promote their books. It doesn't require any sales skills whatsoever.

It really doesn't even matter much if you have any previous experience publishing or marketing. Just about anyone is able to pull this off with a little practice and some common sense. My guess is that if you are publishing your work, you're halfway decent with a pen at least. Assuming that's the case, then you're already set. You have everything you need to get started.

Thanks to the internet, so many things have become easier for the average person to do on their own. Blogs and social media have opened the door to huge audiences waiting to hear what you have to say. Yes, even you. Everyone has a voice these days.

Your job is only to find the right things to say. If you can speak like an authority, you will be regarded as one.

This book is the perfect guide for you if you are just getting started or even if you are a veteran Kindle book publisher. You will learn the secrets of mastering The Amazon Kindle book ecosystem. You will also learn step by step how to "scale" your Kindle book so that you can make more sales and more money. In addition, I will show you how to become an absolute beast when it comes to marketing your Kindle book via the internet and social media. I will turn you into a Kindle book marketing Jedi.

This book is filled with a great deal of resources that you can access immediately. We're also going to cover book promotion tactics like virtual book tours, press release writing etc. that will enable you to effectively brand yourself as an author as well as sell more books.

Most of the methods that are shared in this book are cutting edge and as such can't be found anywhere else because I've never shared them with anyone until now. By the time you have finished reading this book, you will be full of creative and new ideas for promoting, marketing and selling your Kindle book. Feel free to adapt these ideas in whatever ways work best for you.

So without further ado, let's dive in...shall we?

Virtual Book Tours

A neat and innovative way to promote and market your Kindle books is to try going on a virtual book tour. This type of promotion is similar to and involves many of the other methods covered in the subsequent chapters.

Much of the planning that goes into a virtual book tour involves reaching out to bloggers and book reviewers who are willing to feature you on their blogs during your tour. You can think of a virtual book tour as being very similar to a real life publicity tour, which usually means booking appearances at certain bookstores or other locations to promote your new book.

You have two options when it comes to planning a virtual book tour: hiring a company or doing on your own. Think of the first option as being similar to hiring a publicist. They will be in charge of the same types of tasks when it comes to your book tour.

If you choose to hire a company, you should expect them to do some research and find a list of blogs which are a good fit for your book and they should arrange for your virtual appearances on blogs. Usually these types of agreements work out as an exchange of favors, so to speak.

Similar to guest blogging, a virtual book tour is a chance to offer the site owner content of some sort for their readers in exchange for the exposure. This may actually be a guest post, but it could also be an online radio show interview or a podcast as well.

Also sometimes known as "author tours," some writers opt to offer each blog's audience some sort of bonus for purchasing their book or throw in some type of special promotional material.

Generally speaking, there are three main types of virtual book tours. The first is considered the traditional tour, which can last anywhere between one to three weeks. These tours typically include one new appearance each day.

The second type is similar, but lasts several weeks or even months. One way to do this is to pitch the idea of writing a series of posts for one of the blogs in your tour list. Or you can space it out by scheduling one podcast interview for each week of the tour.

The third is the shortest in duration and is sometimes known as a "blast off" campaign as it only runs for a few days, usually less than a week. These types of virtual book tours have been used by some authors to successfully boost their Amazon ranking after recently launching a new title.

For best results when planning a virtual book tour, start compiling your list of appearances and blogs at least two months in advance.

Here are a list of companies who offer virtual book tour services. As always, be sure to do your research before hiring a company for your promotional campaign.

1. Pump Up Your Book (http://www.pumpupyourbookpromotion.com/virtualbooktours.html)
2. Virtual Book Tour Cafe (http://www.virtualbooktourcafe.com/)
3. TLC Book Tours (http://tlcbooktours.com/)
4. Nurture Virtual Book Tourz (http://nurtureyourbooks.com/vbtblog/)

5. Tempting Book Tours
   (http://temptingbooktours.com/)
6. Author Marketing Experts
   (http://www.amarketingexpert.com/blog/)
7. Net Connect Publicity
   (http://www.netconnectpublicity.com/)
8. Novel Publicity (http://www.novelpublicity.com/)
9. Blog Tour Palooza (http://www.bookmarket.com/blog-tour-palooza.htm)
10. Book Festivals (http://bookfestivals.com/)
11. Author's Broadcast
    (http://www.authorsbroadcast.com/)
12. Lit Connect (http://litconnect.com/virtual-book-tours)
13. Author Assistant (http://theyppublishing.com/author-assistant/)
14. Alex Mandossian
    (http://www.alexmandossian.com/tag/virtual-book-tour/)
15. BeWitching Book Tours
    (http://bewitchingbooktours.blogspot.com/)
16. Blog Book Tours (http://blogbooktours.blogspot.com/)
17. Mystical Book Tours
    (http://mysticalbookblogtours.blogspot.com/)
18. LitFuse Publicity (http://litfusegroup.com/campaigns)
19. Enchanted Book Promotions
    (http://enchantedbooktours.eternalised.net/)
20. Sizzling PR (http://sizzlingpr.com/)
21. Book Promotion Services
    (http://bookpromotionservices.com/tour-prices/)
22. JKS Communications
    (http://www.jkscommunications.com/services/)

On the other hand, if you want to take on this type of promotion for your Kindle book independently, then here is the best formula for getting the most out of your virtual book tour.

1. Start researching and finding the right blogs and websites that are likely to welcome your book for an appearance. Be sure the site features other books from within your genre before adding it to your list of possibilities.

2. Assuming you plan a couple months out, then once your list is completed (how many blogs you choose is entirely up to you) you need to start working on a customized email pitch for each individual site in your list. That means no sending a one-size-fits-all template. This won't get you very far, trust me. You need to spend time on each blog you plan on pitching so you have some points of reference when you reach out to them.

3. Work out the booking dates for your appearance on each blog and create a tour calendar.

4. After your tour is complete, be sure to promote the appearances from your own site and through social media as well.

As you can see, none of this is rocket science. It's the type of stuff that anyone is able to do with a little bit of effort. There are a few things to keep in mind while working through the aforementioned process. Let's go over each of them briefly.

When you are writing your email pitch to the bloggers in your list, you should include several pieces of key information. The most important will be a short personal introduction, the title and description for your book, and what you have to offer their blog.

You don't have to limit yourself to offering a guest post. Some bloggers prefer webinar sessions or other forms of interactive content for their readers. Be sure that you include a link to your squeeze page in the email you send. If a blogger agrees to book you for your upcoming tour, then this has the potential to send loads of targeted traffic to your squeeze page.

To help you stay on top of your efforts, you should create a spreadsheet before you start contacting bloggers for your tour. Make columns for the website address of each blog, the name of the blogger or reviewer you are emailing, their email address, the date you first contacted them, the date of their response (if you receive one) and a final column for the date you book with them for your tour (if you land one).

Book Trailers

Think movies are the only art form that can benefit from a visual preview? Think again! Today, tons of authors are experimenting with a new idea: trailers for their books! This is an exciting and effective way to build buzz and awareness of your newest book.

So what exactly is a book trailer? It's a marketing tool that uses visuals to grab the attention of viewers and get them interested enough in your book to click through and purchase a copy so they can get started reading it immediately!

How does one go about creating a book trailer, you might be wondering? Well, the process is fairly involved so don't expect to get this accomplished in a single day. You will need to set aside some time to devote to producing your own video, if that's the route you decide to go.

The main disadvantage for making a book trailer is that unlike movies, you probably don't have any visuals to convey the story that your book tells. What this translates to is finding the right images to use in your trailer, which may be an undertaking all by itself.

As you may already know, you must have permission to use images that you did not create or photograph yourself. In some cases, you even need a model's release to use some photographs. Failing to do this can result in lots of legal trouble, so don't shrug this off and be sure to play by the rules when selecting photos.

One way to find images online that are free to use is by searching for "public domain" photos using Google. This will help you find visuals which don't cost money and which you have the rights to use in your book trailer.

Another great resource for finding royalty-free photos that you can use is Flickr. They have an entire section of the site devoted to "Creative Commons," which is a selection of images that the creators have licensed for use by others.

If you have enough money set aside in your book marketing budget to invest in high quality images, you can try searching royalty-free stock photography sites instead. These all have their own pricing models and types of licenses, so don't spend any money on graphics before reviewing the license to be sure you have the rights to use it in your book trailer.

If creating your own book trailer, you may want to start playing around with Microsoft Movie Maker. Windows 7 comes with this program, and if you spend some time learning how to use all its features then you may be able to pull this off relatively well. For a professional look and feel, be sure to try out different effects for your trailer like fading in from one image to the next.

There are a few common mistakes to avoid when creating a book trailer as well. Too often they include nothing but still shots that don't directly relate to the book's topic and perhaps some music clips that play in the background. This is NOT a book trailer!

Instead, you should go through the following checklist and not skip on any one of these basic requirements for a true book trailer:

- Images, photographs AND at least one short video or animation clip

- At least some text on the screen for part of the trailer (a short quote from an editorial review can work great for this)

- A professional voice over to narrate your trailer

- Music clip

These should be considered the bare minimum for your trailer. Of course, you can always skip out on hiring a pro to record a voice over providing that you own the right equipment and wish to do this part yourself or use someone you know personally.

Another issue is that many music clips are copyrighted, just like a great deal of photographs and images found online. You will want to take the same precautions when selecting music for your trailer as you did when you chose images and photos which you have the right to use.

If tinkering around and editing all of your media elements until you end up with a presentable video is not your thing, you can hire a professional production company to create your book trailer as well. There are several options, as this is becoming quite a popular method of advertising and promoting your book.

Here is a list of some of the most well-known and reputable production companies that currently offer book trailers and other similar services for authors.

Circle of Seven Productions (http://www.cosproductions.com/)

Authorlink (http://www.authorlink.com/about/avproduction.php)

Blazing Trailers (http://www.blazingtrailers.com/submit.php)

Living Jacket (http://livingjacket.com/)

Book Shorts, Inc. (http://www.movingstories.tv/about/)

Writer's Direct (http://www.writersdirect.net/services/book-trailers/)

Dog Ear Publishing (http://dogearpublishing.net/book-marketing-services/marketing-book-trailers.php)

Red 14 Films (http://red14films.com/)

Book Video Creation (http://www.bookvideocreation.com/)

NoWiki Productions (http://www.nowickiproductions.com/)

Apremount Productions (http://apremontproductions.com/book_trailers)

Suzie Design (http://www.design.suzannahsafi.com/)

One of the most important tasks that a professional book trailer company will take care of on your behalf is distribution of your trailer. Any company whose services are worth your investment will be sure to promote your book trailer on sites like Youtube and a long list of other social video sharing sites.

In addition to the more popular video sites, there are also several websites devoted to book trailers, believe it or not. In fact, once your video is created you can submit it to such sites on your own if you have time or think it might be a worthwhile effort.

Here are a few select websites and blogs that accept book trailer submissions:

BookTrailers.net (http://www.book-trailers.net/2007/08/how-to-submit-book-trailer.html)

Comic Book Trailers (http://www.comicbooktrailers.com/faq/)

Clean Book Trailers (http://cleanbooktrailers.blogspot.com/)

Journey to Self-Publishing (http://www.journeytoselfpublishing.com/?p=220) – Christian books only

If Books Could Talk (http://bookvideos.wordpress.com/)

Bookcaster (http://bookcaster.com/)

Book and Trailer Showcase (http://booktrailershowcase.com/advertise-with-bts/contact/)

Book Riot (http://bookriot.tv/submit-a-trailer/)

Watch the Book (http://www.watchthebook.com/)

TrailerSpy (http://www.trailerspy.com/book-trailers/)

So while book trailers are not for every author, they can be worth exploring if you happen to be among the more innovative crowd or like to try new methods of promotion. Keep in mind that the average length of a book trailer is around three minutes, and it's not advised to let your trailer run much longer than this.

Also, book trailers seem to be equally as effective for non-fiction and fiction novels alike. So if you decide to skip out on this technique, don't use your genre as the reason!

Promoting Your Book In Forums

Just like any other type of product, whether virtual or physical, books and ebooks can be effectively promoted by active participation in online forums. However, this method of promoting your book should be approached with some caution, as it's easy to accidentally stumble and end up being banned from a forum.

In general, forum marketing is relatively similar regardless of what it is that you have to promote. They are considered virtual communities where like minded individuals gather and discuss their shared interests, whatever the topic of the forum may be.

They are not advertising space and they tend to not take too kindly to shameless self-promotion either. These are two things to keep fresh in your mind if you plan on participating in any author forums.

Be sure to carefully review the rules for each and every forum you sign up for and decide to join in the conversation. You may not realize that some do not allow posting links, even ones for which you are not affiliated or connected to in any way. There are various reasons that forum moderators decide to put these rules in place, but the ultimate result of ignoring them or not knowing they exist, is being banned.

Assuming that a forum allows you to post links, the best place for one is usually in your forum signature. This oftentimes includes your name and a link, which appears beneath each of your posts within a forum. Think of this as being similar to an email signature, since that's essentially what it acts as.

Don't assume that links are acceptable in your signature either though, as each forum has their own unique rules where that is concerned as well. For example, some forums allow only a certain number of lines for use in your signature. Some allow images within signs, while some do not.

Since forums are communities, they are very sensitive to violations of their rules. Even if you escape with a warning rather than a ban, you won't be welcomed by the other members if you start off on the wrong foot. So it might be a good idea to lurk for a bit before deciding to speak up.

Here is a list of some popular forums for authors and writers who would like to get extra exposure for their books and use subtle promotion methods to increase awareness of their work.

The Book Marketing Network (http://thebookmarketingnetwork.com/)

Kindle Forum (http://kindleforum.co/)

Published Authors (http://www.publishedauthors.org/)

Writers.Net (http://www.writers.net/forum/)

Every Author (http://www.everyauthor.com/forum/)

World Literary Cafe
(http://www.worldliterarycafe.com/forum/35)

Kindle Boards (http://www.kindleboards.com/)

Book Summit
(http://www.booksummit.com/forum/categories/main-kindle-forum/)

Kindle Central
(http://forums.kindlecentral.com/forums/index.jspa)

Absolute Write Water Cooler
(http://www.absolutewrite.com/forums/forumdisplay.php?f=47)

All Things Publishing and Self-Publishing
(http://forums.nathanbransford.com/viewforum.php?f=5)

The Self-Publishing Review
(http://www.selfpublishingreview.com/)

The most important thing about marketing your books in forums is to treat it like social media – be subtle at all times. Add value to the conversation before you start trying to sell something to the members of the community.

Blogging and Guest Blogging

This is going to be one of the most important areas of marketing and promoting your books as an author. Why? Because bloggers are going to be the people who provide you with one of the most valuable aspects of book marketing you will chase as a writer: book reviews!

As a self-published author, you have a distinct disadvantage over traditionally published writers when it comes to attracting big names to check out your work and write reviews. That's just not going to happen. So it's a good thing that the changes in the industry have given bloggers a voice every bit as powerful as some of the biggest names in book reviewers and critics.

The fact is that book bloggers are the people with opinions that others listen to. They manage entire websites that specialize in reviewing new books and ebooks, even from brand new first-time authors like yourself.

This is a huge opportunity for you to gain some attention for your book and spread the word. The great news is that it's easy to do too! If you have any people skills at all, you will do just fine at this. Even if you are lacking in that area, it really helps that you will be corresponding with them online, which is much easier than in person for some of us.

It's a good idea to start researching potential book bloggers several months before you intend to publish your book. This will also help you plan a virtual book tour as well. The first step is to start searching for book review blogs that cover your genre and to start following them.

Once you've spotted a potential blog that may review your book or ebook, then you should add it to your ongoing list of bloggers to pitch via email. There are three things which you MUST do before contacting a reviewer:

1. Read their review policy in full. Don't waste their time. These people offer to review books for free because they enjoy reading specific genres. In fact, you will be wasting your time as well if you pitch a reviewer of YA fiction when you've written a non-fiction book about customer service. Be courteous and professional and always read the entire review policy.

2. Read a minimum of two reviews already posted on the site by the reviewer you are planning to pitch. This will give you a better idea of what types of books they like and don't like. Try to find a positive review and a negative one, so you get a balanced sampling of their opinions.

   If you don't like the style of their negative reviews, maybe you should reconsider pitching them if you don't want to risk getting a bad review. Keep in mind that these are honest reviews written by people you don't know. It's not the same thing as getting a review by your friends or family members, who are likely to say only good things about your writing.

   This is a real review, so proceed with as much caution as you think is wise. The point here is to acquaint yourself with the reviewer well enough that you feel secure asking them to review your book.

3. This third item is actually optional, but recommended as a sign of common courtesy and good manners. Since you're asking for something free, it's a nice gesture to offer a copy of the book so that the reviewer is able to read it without having to spend any money.

    Oftentimes they will take you up on this offer, but some prefer to purchase their own copy so they don't have to disclose to their readers that they received compensation for the review in the form of a free book (yes, that is considered a material connection and under FTC regulations, this information is supposed to be disclosed on websites and blogs).

Guest blogging is a very effective method of increasing traffic to your own website (where you can definitely promote all of your books) and becoming more known amid the blogosphere, both as an author and a blogger.

Some people think guest blogging is tough to break into, but that's not really true. While it's actually quite simple and relatively easy, it does require a certain amount of patience and effort. Let's elaborate on that a bit for a moment.

As you're starting your search for book review blogs, be sure to leave comments in the reviews you read on all of the ones you plan to pitch. Don't just write something meaningless like "Great review, can't wait to read this book!"

That isn't going to cut it. Make useful comments that add to the conversation. A better example would be "This really reminds me of _____, which I enjoyed quite a bit. Being a big fan of paranormal romance novels, this sounds like something worth checking out for sure. Since I don't mind a book that needs a little editing, I think I'll make this next on my reading list."

Of course, that's just an example. The point is that you address the specifics mentioned in the review. Reference the genre, acknowledge the flaws mentioned, relate it to something else that you have read and enjoyed. Comment on more than one or two reviews.

The idea here is to become a regular commenter on these blogs. This will warm up your leads when you get ready to pitch guest posts to the bloggers who manage them.

Also, spend some time finding blogs about writing and do the same thing with these. Unless you want to write book reviews, this will probably be a better avenue for guest posting.

Once the blogger knows you by name and has responded to your useful comments, they will be a much warmer lead when you present them with the idea of submitting a guest post to them.

Pitch them via email in much the same way as you did the reviewers, but make it more about them and their blog than about you and your idea, or your book. Just briefly introduce yourself and mention being a long time reader.

Make it clear that you are familiar with the types of posts they regularly feature and ask them what type of posts they are most interested in at that time. You can throw in a line or two explaining that you are an author and what your experience is with writing, but there isn't much of a need to mention your books by title unless asked.

Typically, most blogs allow you to write a byline that appears beneath your guest post, telling the readers who you are and where they can find more of your stuff. The byline is usually only a couple lines, so use it wisely. The majority of blogs only allow one or two links at most within the byline, such as one for your website and one for your Twitter profile.

Writing Your Email Pitch

When you have a good sized list of potential reviewers lined up, it's time to write an email pitch and start making contact with these people. There are a few things to keep in mind which are very important, so don't ignore any of the tips in this list. Follow each step exactly and you will be sure to get at least a few positive responses.

Step One: Write the body of your email and save the text as a template. The body of your email is a short paragraph to introduce yourself as an author and include a quick mention of your book's title. The second paragraph should expand on your book without going into too much detail. Tell the reviewer what genre your book falls into, what it is about and why you think it might interest them. Link to your Amazon product page in this email as well.

Step Two: Personalize each and every email that you plan to send to a reviewer. This means taking your body template and adding a couple lines before and after it. The lines before the body should address the reviewer by name, whenever possible. You should mention their site or blog by name and tell them how you found them.

The more details you offer about their blog, the more serious they will take your request. The lines after the body should include a short call to action and a polite closing with your signature. Offer to provide a copy of the book if they are interested in checking it out, tell them where it can be purchased online and end by letting them know that you are looking forward to their response.

Step Three: Remember earlier in this guide we mentioned starting a spreadsheet to track all of your book marketing efforts? Well it's time to pull that spreadsheet up and start adding reviewers to your list once you've sent your first email to them. This will help you keep track of which blogs you've made contact with already and which ones responded with a yes or no on your request for a review.

Step Four: Follow up and thank reviewers. This one is important. If you don't get a response from a blogger, it's acceptable to send a follow up email after a week or so. If you don't hear back after the second email, it's safe to assume they either are too busy to consider reading your book or they are not interested. Time to move on.

For those who do agree to review your book, most of them will offer you an approximate date. While you shouldn't hold them to it, it's okay to follow up with them if they haven't posted the review within a week of the date they first gave you. Just send a friendly email to touch base, asking how they are enjoying your book so far.

Don't be pushy and don't send another email if you don't hear back. When a reviewer posts a review of your book, be sure to follow up with a thank you email to express your appreciation. This is a great way to make new friends in the blogosphere and network with other writers.

Finding Blogs To Review Your Book

While you probably won't have any luck scoring a review in a big media name like the New York Times, there are still plenty of smaller book review blogs that have wide readerships and can do a great deal in terms of promotion and marketing for your book.

So how do you find the right blogs for your book? Here is a list of some popular book review sites that get a good amount of traffic and post reviews on a regular basis. These sites review fiction genres, but check their review policies to see if they review your specific type of story.

100 Fiction Book Review Blogs

1. About Happy Books (www.abouthappybooks.com)
2. An Abundance of Books (http://anabundanceofbooks.blogspot.com)
3. The "A" - Jurnale (http://the-a-jurnale.blogspot.com)
4. Alaskan Bookie (http://alaskanbookie.blogspot.com)
5. Alchemy of Scrawl (http://alchemyofscrawl.wordpress.com)
6. Alexa Loves Books (http://alexalovesbooks.blogspot.com)
7. Alexia's Chronicles (http://alexiachronicles.blogspot.com)
8. Ali's Bookshelf (http://alisbookshelfreviews.blogspot.com)
9. All Booked Up (http://allbookedup-elena.blogspot.com)
10. All I Ever Read (http://books.nicoleabouttown.com)
11. All Metaphor (http://allmetaphor.com)
12. All That Shaz (http://allthatshazzer.blogspot.com)
13. All Things Books (http://speedyreader-allthingsbooks.blogspot.com)
14. Always Reading (http://alwaysreading.net)
15. Always With a Book (http://alwayswithabook.blogspot.com)
16. Amy's Books & Writing Den (http://amysbooksden.blogspot.com)
17. An Author's Tale (http://anauthorstale.blogspot.com)
18. An Irregular Silsbee (http://irregularsilsbee.blogspot.com)

19. And The Plot Thickens… (http://and-the-plot-thickens.blogspot.com)

20. Angel Thoughts (http://www.angelgraham.blogspot.com)

21. Anglers Rest (http://anglersrest.blogspot.com)

22. Aobibliosphere (http://aobibliosphere.blogspot.com)

23. Armchair Archives (http://armchairarchives.blogspot.com)

24. As I Turn the Pages (http://asiturnthepages.blogspot.com

25. As the Crowe Fllies & Reads (http://asthecrowefliesandreads.blogspot.com)

26. Assortments (http://www.blogonlinerandom.blogspot.com)

27. Auntie Spinelli's Thought Corner (http://geobobspinelli.blogspot.com)

28. Author Exposure (http://www.authorexposure.com)

29. Badyne (http://badyne.blogspot.com)

30. Babies, Books & Signs (http://www.babiesbooksandsigns.blogspot.com)

31. BaffledBooks (http://baffledbooks.com)

32. Baja Greenawalt's Cozy Book Nook (http://baja-greenawalts-cozybooknook.blogspot.com/)

33. Basically books (http://basicallybooks1994.blogspot.com/)

34. Bay State Reader's Advisory (http://baystatera.com)

35. Bea's Book Nook (http://beasbooknook.blogspot.com)

36. Belle's Bookshelf (http://bellesbookshelf.blogspot.com/)

37. Beloved Literature (http://belovedliterature.com/)

38. Best books (http://bestbooks1.blogspot.com/)

39. Between The Lines Book Reviews (http://betweenthelines–bookreviews.blogspot.com)

40. Bex (http://www.anarmchairbythesea.blogspot.com)

41. Bibliofreak.net – A Book Review Blog(http://www.bibliofreak.net)

42. Bibliophagista: Better Read Than Dead (http://bibliophagista.blogspot.com)

43. Bibliophile Mystery (http://bibliophilemystery.blogspot.com/)

44. Bibliophile's Corner (http://bibliophilescorner.blogspot.com)

45. The Bibliophilic Book Blog (http://www.bibliophilicbookblog.com/)

46. Bibliosaurus Text (http://www.bibliosaurustext.com)

47. Big Book Little Book Reviews (http://bigbooklittlebook.blogspot.com)

48. Birdbrain(ed) Book Blog (http://birdbrainbb.net)

49. Bitch Lit Blog (http://bitchlitblog.wordpress.com)

50. Can't Put It Down (http://www.readitreviewit.wordpress.com)

51. Capricious Reader (http://www.capriciousreader.com)

52. Carmen's Book Adventure (http://carmensbookadventure.blogspot.com/)

53. A Casual Reader's Blog (http://ellsey.blogspot.com)

54. Catering to the Life of the Mind (http://caterlotm.blogspot.com)

55. Cathy's Reading List (http://cathysreadinglist.blogspot.com)

56. Cat's Thoughts (http://www.thinkingcatblog.com/)

57. Ceinwenn's Book Ramblings (http://ceinwenn.wordpress.com)

58. CentralCaliGrrrl (http://centralcaligrrrl.blogspot.com/)

59. Cerebral Girl in a Redneck World (http://cerebralgirl.blogspot.com/)

60. Chachic's Book Nook (http://chachic.wordpress.com/)

61. Chaos, Coffee, & a Bookshelf (http://www.chaoscoffeeandabookshelf.com)

62. Chocoholic Bookie (http://www.chocoholicbookie.com)

63. Christa's Hooked on Books (http://christashookedonbooks.blogspot.com)

64. Chronicles of an Enamored Soul (http://ibetuthinkthisblogisaboutyou.blogspot.com/)

65. Cindy Swanson (http://cindysbookclub.blogspot.com)

66. Clandestine Sanctuary (http://cladestinesanctuary.blogspot.com/)

67. clairexxoxo (http://life-as-a-newbie.blogspot.com)

68. closetreader (http://www.closetreader.com/)

69. Coffee and a Book Chick (http://www.coffeeandabookchick.com)

70. The Coffee Pot (http://freshcoffeespot.blogspot.com)

71. Colloquium (http://www.jhsiess.com)

72. Confessions of a Common Reader (http://confessionsofacommonreader.wordpress.com/)

73. Coreena McBurnie (http://coreenamcburnie.blogspot.com)

74. The Cottage Bookshelf (http://thecottagebookshelf.blogspot.com/)

75. A Cozy Reader's Corner (http://acozyreaderscorner.blogspot.com)

76. CSI:Librarian (http://csilibrarian.wordpress.com/)

77. Curiosity Killed The Bookworm (http://curiositykilledthebookworm.blogspot.com)

78. Curled Up With a Good Book and a Cup of Tea (http://goodbooksandacupoftea.blogspot.com)

79. Curling Up By The fire (http://www.curlingupbythefire.blogspot.com)

80. Curling Up With a Good Book (http://www.curlingupwithagoodbook.com)

81. Cynical Bookworm (http://cynicalbookworm.blogspot.com/)

82. Darlene's Book Nook (http://darlenesbooknook.blogspot.com/)

83. DD The Book Slut's Blog (http://ddthebookslut.wordpress.com/)

84. Demure Connoisseur (http://demureconnoisseur.blogspot.com/)

85. Devourer of Books (http://www.devourerofbooks.com)

86. Diary of a Writer in Progress (http://diaryofawriterinprogress.blogspot.com/)

87. A Discovery of Books (http://adiscoveryofbooks.blogspot.com/)

88. Does It Really Matter? (http://www.dgr8mom.com/)

89. Dog-Eared & Bookmarked (http://dog-earedandbookmarked.blogspot.com/)

90. Dolce Bellezza (http://www.dolcebellezza.net)

91. The Dreamers' Disease (http://the-dreamers-disease.blogspot.com/)

92. Drey's library (http://dreyslibrary.blogspot.com)

93. Earth's Book Nook (www.earthsbooknook.blogspot.com)

94. Eastern Sunset Reads (http://easternsunset-reads.blogspot.com/)

95. Eclectic Reader Book Review (http://eclecticbooks.wordpress.com/)

96. The Eloquent Page (http://www.theeloquentpage.co.uk)

97. Endless Reading (http://www.endlessreading.blogspot.com)

98. Erin Reads (http://erinreads.com)

99. Escape Reality, Read Fiction! (http://www.readingreality.net)

100.   Kathryn's Book Nook (http://www.kathrynsbooknook.wordpress.com)

If you would like to have more fiction book review blogs to contact I have a more extensive list available that consists of a total of 1,300 book review blogs. To obtain that list just visit:

http://www.makeprofitsnow.com/bloglist.html

Finding Opportunities for Publicity & Author Promotion

There are tons of different ways you can score extra publicity as an author and find ways to subtly promote your books to a large audience of interested readers and listeners. One of the best ways to increase your exposure and brand yourself as an author is to land interviews on radio shows, podcasts and even as a guest blogger on other similar websites. We're going to expand on each one of these ideas in the following sections.

Radio Shows, Podcasts & Interviews

Finding radio shows and podcasts that are looking for guests is done in much the same way that we explained how to find book review bloggers. You can try some of the sites that I'm about to mention here to search for any shows or podcasts that regularly feature author interviews to start with.

Also, keep in mind that there are lots of different types of shows that you might appeal to as an author. The assumption working in your favor is that you are an expert on a topic. Whether you write fiction or non-fiction, you know the craft of writing professionally and people will be interested in what you have to say.

Granted, you may have a slight advantage in this particular area if you are a non-fiction writer. The reason for this is simple. Non-fiction is easier to tie into current events or closely related topics that the public are interested in at any given time.

Keep in mind that memoirs and autobiographical types of books are not works of fiction. This means that if you have written a book about your own life, then you have a point of reference for speaking on any of the things which have happened both in the story and in your life.

For example, let's say you wrote a memoir about a time in your life when you worked as a lifeguard. You probably have tons of interesting stories about saving people's lives and as an author, you are now viewed as an expert on safe swimming. That happens to be a topic that has wide appeal, and it can be tied into a huge number of different themes that shows may have. Here is a list of places where you can search for shows.

Radio Guest List (http://www.radioguestlist.com)

The Author Show (http://www.wnbnetworkwest.com/WnbAuthorsShow.html)

Artist First (http://www.artistfirst.com)

Blog Talk Radio (http://www.blogtalkradio.com)

Talking Books TV (http://talkingbookstv.com)

BookPage (http://bookpage.com/content/contact-us)

Authors On Tour (http://authorsontourlive.com)

The Writing Show (http://www.writingshow.com/)

Interview Tips for Radio, Podcasts & More

Keep in mind that you can also pitch radio shows and other outlets who may be interested in doing an interview for their show. Remember that you are also offering them something, rather than asking for a handout. You get the publicity, and they get a guest for their show.

It's important to take note of a few things before you dive into doing interviews though. Let's cover some of the most basic yet important details.

- Since most shows will be having you as a guest remotely, you will probably be using a phone. Avoid using a cell phone, since these can get bad reception and are not very reliable if you have agreed to be a guest on a radio show, especially if the show is having you on live.

  Some shows are syndicated and record in advance, which means they can be edited later. But if you're live, then you don't want to risk cutting out while the interview is taking place.

- Get all the details ahead of time and mark your calendar on the day you have been booked. If you're doing a phone interview, make sure that you have a quiet place to take the call and try to eliminate any background noise that may make it difficult for the host to hear you when you are answering questions.

- Relax and stay calm. Some people get incredibly anxious over doing this type of thing, but it's really not as scary as it might seem beforehand. Just pretend you are on the phone with a friend from work. Stay professional, but don't be too rigid.

  If you're worried about how to answer any questions, you can always suggest some questions to the host before the date of the interview. There is no guarantee that they will use your ideas, but they are likely to at least get a vague idea of what you are willing to talk about.

- Figure out how you will obtain a copy of the interview to include on your own website afterward. Ask the producer if they will be able to send you an mp3 copy, which is usually pretty easy for them to do. Otherwise, just use a recording tool of your own. You can use the interview on your website where you feature your recent press and media coverage. Video interviews work great too, if you can find any blogs or shows that use Skype to conduct interviews.

In closing, just try your best to be creative when you approach anyone to be a guest on their blog, their show or whatever it is that they are putting on. It's their show, not yours. This means that they already have an audience who has some expectations and they may be willing to have you on as a guest, but you are probably going to have to adapt to the right tone and style for their particular show.

Writing & Distributing Press Releases

Writing a press release is one of the most important things to do when you go to publish your book, hands down. If distributed properly, it will help you generate publicity and open the door for tons of media opportunities all on its own.

So how do you write a press release for a book? It's pretty simple. If you have never written a press release before, then you need to become familiar with the standards and format expected of a press release.

You may want to spend some time researching how press release writing is done before diving in, but here are some general instructions:

1. Write a killer headline. Since most people skim through headlines searching for things that jump out at them, your headline is one of the most important parts of the entire press release. You need to focus on getting people's attention with your headline.

Reporters and other individuals in the media are not easily impressed, making it especially difficult to get them interested. You need to be unique and different, you must stand out from the crowd. Even if you are writing about something that many consider boring, you must get creative and find a way to make it sound worth reading or learning more about. As for formatting, the headline should always be written in title case.

2. Back it up with a strong sub-headline to add more details. Take this as an opportunity to follow up with some extra information, but stick to keeping it interesting. The goal of the headline and sub headline is to reel the reader in so that they read the rest of your press release.

3. Answer the basic questions in the lead. The next part of your press release is the lead, which typically addresses all the particular details of your story. Tell who the story is about, what they have done, where they are located and other information.

4. Tell the story using the body of your press release. This is where you want to include all the most important info related to your story. As an author, you could make comparisons between your style and other famous authors that inspire your writing. Try to tie it into some hot topic in the media or news at the time of writing. The body usually includes 2-4 short paragraphs and normally includes a quote somewhere within it from a key person involved in the news story (in this case, probably you!)

5. Last comes the boilerplate, similar to a byline. The boilerplate is the last part of your press release and is kind of like a byline when you guest blog. It's sort of an "about us" section that is typically four to five sentences long.

6. Always write your press releases in third person. Remember that a press release is something that an author's publicist would probably be in charge of writing. Not all writers can afford a publicist though, so there is nothing wrong with writing your own as long as you stick to the third person.

Also, it's naturally best to keep your tone objective throughout the press release. You don't want to give yourself glowing praise or seem like you're trying to hype things up to make sales. This is totally the wrong way to approach press releases. This isn't a sales letter, it's a form of subtle promotion and should be used accordingly.

7. A final note on formatting. At the end of your press release, you should always add the number symbol three times in a row with no spaces on a separate line. This is standard formatting for press releases and helps them to determine the end of your story. It would look like this ###, but it would be on its own line.

Of course, if you're not feeling confident enough to write your own press release, there are tons of services that will gladly write one for you in exchange for a fee. In fact, many press release distribution sites also offer writing services if you have the budget and aren't sure you can write one on your own.

Distributing Your Press Release to the Media

There are tons of sites online where you can submit your press release, some paid and others free. To maximize your results, you should probably submit to as many free ones as you can and also consider investing in a paid service to distribute them.

There is nothing wrong with free press release submission sites, and we have included a long list of them for you to submit to in this section. Some of the sites listed are also paid services, such as PRWeb.

The advantage to using a paid service is that the company will send your press release to thousands of media contacts that the company has worked to develop. More journalists and reporters will see your news story this way, and they will take it more seriously because they trust the company you have paid to handle distribution.

Most paid press release sites (and even some of the free ones) manually review each and every press release they receive before they approve it and send it out. A paid service basically guarantees that your press release gets tons more visibility and it can be a great way to attract interested radio show producers looking for interviews and many other people who would like to offer an opportunity to share your expertise.

List of Press Release Submission Sites

PR Web (http://www.prweb.com)
PR Log (http://www.prlog.org)
eReleases (http://www.ereleases.com)

PR News Lead (http://www.prnewslead.com)

Online PR News (http://www.onlineprnews.com)

Press Release 365 (http://www.pressrelease365.com)

Express Press Release Distribution (http://express-press-release.net)

24-7 Press Release (http://www.24-7pressrelease.com)

PR Newswire (http://www.prnewswire.com)

WebWire (http://www.webwire.com)

iNewswire (http://www.inewswire.com)

Marketwire (http://www.marketwire.com)

PR Leap (http://www.prleap.com)

PressWire (http://www.presswire.com)

PR Buzz (http://www.prbuzz.com)

My PR Genie (http://www.myprgenie.com)

Real Wire (http://www.realwire.com)

PR Nine (http://www.prnine.com)

Press King (http://www.pressking.com)

PR Free (http://www.prfree.com)

PR Zoom (http://www.przoom.com)

Press Release Circle (http://www.pressreleasecircle.com)

Press Release Sender (http://www.pressreleasesender.com)

Source Wire (http://www.sourcewire.com)

Blurb Point (http://www.blurbpoint.co.uk)

Free Press Release Center (http://www.freepressreleasecenter.com)

Press Method (http://www.pressmethod.com)

Press Release Point (http://www.pressreleasepoint.com)

Free Press Index (http://www.freepressindex.com)

Submit Free PR (http://www.submitfreepr.com)

1888PressRelease (http://www.1888pressrelease.com)

Wide PR (http://www.widepr.com)

PR Blue (http://www.prblue.com)

Release Wire (http://www.releasewire.org)

Send 2 Press (http://www.send2press.com)

PR Underground (http://www.prunderground.com)

eWorld Wire (http://www.eworldwire.com)

Online PR News (http://www.onlineprnews.com)

EZ PR (http://www.ezpr.org)

Submit Press Release 123
(http://www.submitpressrelease123.com)

Using Social Media to Promote Your Books

Social media is not a new topic, and you've probably read dozens of articles outlining the benefits of using social sites to promote your business, or in this case, your books. Not all authors are salespeople or marketers, and oftentimes they want little or nothing to do with the promotion process.

However, social media offers a unique and fun opportunity to engage with your readers and nurture your leads without being a pushy salesperson. In fact, social sites are an author's best friend in this regard.

In the following sections, we'll cover some creative and simple ways you can use different social platforms in your book marketing strategy.

Twitter Promotion for Authors

Twitter is one of the most popular social sites in the world, next to Facebook. Although you might not immediately see the value of sharing one-hundred and forty character status updates with the world, there are a ton of ways to harness the social power of Twitter to brand yourself as an author and promote your books at the same time.

Remember that your Twitter username should be the title of your book or your author name, in most cases. The reason for this is that it will customize the URL for your profile, so that it looks like this: www.twitter.com/booktitle or www.twitter.com/authorname. This makes it easy for prospective followers to find and identify you.

If you're new to Twitter, here are some technical tips for how to use the site effectively:

Use hashtags. Hashtags are words with the number symbol tacked on to the beginning. They look #like this. This is a great way to organize and group your tweets based on the different types you post to your Twitter account. Use them to identify which tweets are about what.

Reply to tweets about your book by using the @ symbol before the name of the user to which you are responding. Start your tweet with @username to address your response to the right person.

Be sure to make good use of the right keywords when tweeting anything about or related to your book. If you have written a paranormal romance, for example, then include those keywords in your tweets and it will be easier for people to find them.

By using both hashtags and appropriate keywords, your tweets have a better chance of showing up in real time search results that Google serves up, which can bring you tons of exposure and search traffic.

Twitter is a great place to share relevant links with your followers. Just keep an even balance of links from outside sources and your own stuff, so that you don't come off as overly promotional. Try to choose links that are both relevant and popular, to increase your retweet rate.

Use Twitter's search feature to find out what sort of topics and issues people are tweeting about within your niche, then try posting helpful solutions that your book or writing may offer them!

Remember to tweet your best stuff more than once. Since Twitter is flooded with new updates around the clock, most of your followers will never see your best tweets if you only tweet them once. Some people on Twitter follow hundreds of users, which means your most awesome stuff could be difficult for them to see unless you post your tweets more than once per day, using different names and accounts.

For a full author branding effect, you should customize your profile in all the areas possible. This includes your bio, avatar and even your background image. Your Twitter background should include the same visual branding you use on other social sites, such as a photo of yourself or a logo design.

Be sure to also include your website address and links to other social profiles. Even though users can't click on them, they can enter them manually to find you in other areas of the web and will do so if they are interested in what you have to say. Obviously it works best to keep these URLs as short as you can, since they will take up space in your background design.

If you're planning an upcoming promotion for your book, try offering your followers a discount code to generate more interest. If you want to measure the success of your Twitter promo efforts, then try tweeting a code to your followers and ask them to enter it when they go to complete a transaction. Keep it simple, like TWEET100 or whatever makes the most sense for your special deal.

If you use other sites like Facebook, LinkedIn and Google+, be sure to link up your Twitter account with your profiles on these sites so that your tweets will appear on all of your profiles for effective cross-promotion.

Update all of your marketing materials so that they include your Twitter username. This means business cards, newsletters, email and forum signatures, the works!

Never use software to automate your Tweets. Twitter was designed for people to share real information, from real people. Bots don't do a very good job of this, and it shows.

Try using some of the most popular Twitter directories if you need to find the right people to build your following. A couple examples of Twitter directories are JustTweetIt and Twello. Use these to identify prospective followers and also to find influencers in your niche for you to follow and retweet.

If you have a large following on Facebook and need to get started on Twitter, just try posting a status update to inform your friends that they can now follow you on Twitter as well.

While Twitter does have a built-in link shortening utility, you should use one like Bit.ly or Goo.gl since you can better track the number of clicks for each link you share using one of these services.

140 characters doesn't seem like much, especially when you are a writer with something to say. However, try to make it a habit to get the point across in a single tweet and avoid letting your message spill into multiple tweets. Doing this makes it very difficult for all of your followers to understand what you are trying to say, or read them in the correct sequence.

Disregard all of the "get twitter followers" schemes that are out there. It might seem like a great idea to get hundreds of new followers, but if it sounds too good to be true, it usually is. This is no exception.

Even if they deliver on the followers, these people are not at all likely to care about your books or be interested in your work as an author. Remember that it's much more valuable to have a small number of followers with high levels of interest than it is to have tons of followers who could care less.

Don't forget to leave enough space in your tweets for others to retweet them. Leave two to three spaces, plus the number of characters in your Twitter username. Others will start the retweet with RT @yourusername.

Since Twitter is all about interaction with followers, be sure to thank people when they retweet or share your tweets by using the @ reply + their username. In fact, it's a great idea to respond ANY time you see a mention of your name or book titles at all. Just remember that big name authors often don't reply to fans or critics, so you will achieve a more personal connection by doing so and it will make you seem more human to your readers.

While Twitter does have a setting that allows you to protect your Tweets, there is really no reason to use the site at all if you are not going to share openly through your account. It's not advised to do this, as it will defeat the purpose of using social media altogether.

Just like it's a good idea to respond to positive comments about you or your writing, it's equally important to address negative feedback shared on Twitter as well. It's not always easy to maintain composure when someone attacks us or delivers some harsh criticism to the writing that we put so much work into, but it's very important to remain professional when responding to negative tweets.

Get the most out of your Twitter experience by using your smartphone to tweet throughout the day, rather than waiting until you are in front of a computer to join in the conversation.

Try your best to strike a mostly even balance between the types of tweets you post to Twitter. That means plenty of retweets, @ replies and original tweets as well. Too much of any one of these is going to work against you.

In the beginning, you may find that retweeting good content from others and promoting outside sources may work better as it comes across as more genuine. Once you've built up your own following and established yourself as a known expert in your niche, then you can slip in an occasional tweet promoting your own stuff.

Looking for a simple and efficient way to keep track of every tweet that mentions your name or book titles? Using Twitter's search feature will show you all the recent tweets for both of these, and as you scroll through them to reply, you can also mark them as favorites if you want to return later and respond after you think about it a bit.

Adding tweets as favorites will make it easy to retrieve them in the future, and is a great way to make sure all your mentions are addressed at some point, even if you don't have time right away.

If you're a fiction author, try occasionally tweeting as one of your main characters or the most popular character from one of your stories. This spices things up and really tends to get fans excited. If you have an ongoing series of fiction books, you may even consider starting a separate account for your main character or heroine. Fans of your stories will be guaranteed followers and will hang onto every word you tweet using this account.

Setup saved searches for your full name and the title of your book or books. When someone tweets that they are reading your book on their Kindle device, take a moment to ask them how they like it so far by using the @ symbol, followed by their twitter username. This really inspires true fans and is a great way to gently encourage book reviews as well!

Tweet teaser content or links to free chapter downloads for your followers to check out. Be sure to link to a squeeze page with an opt-in form to collect email addresses and build your list while delivering free content and samples which make your readers curious and interested.

Facebook Promotion for Authors

Facebook is hands-down the most popular social network on the planet. They may be one of the only viable competitors to internet giants like Google and search engine technology in general. For this reason alone, we don't want to neglect this social platform and it's important to take full advantage of the branding and marketing resources it has to offer.

In addition to creating a personal profile, be sure to setup a Facebook page for your titles or your author brand. Post links to your landing pages, website and blog and share teaser content similar to what you share on sites like Twitter.

Join relevant Facebook groups. If you're a thriller writer, search for groups of people who fit into this category as well. Network with others who write within your genre. Build new relationships with fellow authors and readers alike. They can make outstanding brand ambassadors when you go to launch your next book!

Create polls to ask your readers questions and conduct basic market research right from your Facebook account!

Share links to media interviews, reviews of your book and other press coverage you receive.

If you have a marketing budget for promoting your book, you could experiment with Facebook pay-per-click advertising. Craft an enticing headline and target your ad by several demographics, such as age, country and gender.

If you're a non-fiction author, you can use your Facebook page as a hub for offering your expertise and professional advice. Start a forum where readers and visitors can ask questions directly related to the topic of your ebooks and take the time to provide meaningful answers.

Pinterest Promotion for Authors

Pinterest is the newest addition to the big name players in social media. For being relatively new to the scene, Pinterest has seen monumental growth in a short period of time. While the site is predominantly used by women, there are several ways you can use it to market yourself as an author and promote your books, no matter the genre.

In many ways, Pinterest is like a cross between an image bookmarking service and Twitter. There are tons of similarities between Twitter and Pinterest, so much of your promotional efforts will be similar between the two.

This includes the most basic stuff, such as adding a Pinterest button to your websites, choosing a username consistent with your author branding and having conversations by using the @ symbol to reply to other users.

There are a few neat things you can also do which are more unique to Pinterest. Did you know, for example, that you can setup a board and choose which users can contribute pins? Look for the "Who can pin?" setting when you create your next board and be sure to select "Me + Contributors" to make a collaborative pinboard.

Want to take a peek at all the content from your own website that other users have pinned? Just copy and paste the following URL: http://www.pinterest.com/source/yourusernamehere. Of course, replace the last part with your actual username.

As for image sizes, there is no limit for vertical dimensions on Pinterest. However, the horizontal width is automatically resized to 554 pixels. Don't forget that Pinterest allows you to pin video content to your boards as well, so be sure to pin any book trailers for your titles in your boards!

Just like on all other social sites, you should make effective use of keywords and hashtags related to your books or author brand. Also, you can include links to your website in the description field for each pin you submit to the site, driving traffic and increasing visibility.

Create a biographical pinboard for author branding. Think of this pinboard as your visual autobiography and author resume. Include personal photos, blog snippets, eBook covers, book reviews, media interviews and anything else that relates to your work as an author.

Create individual pinboards for each one of your titles. What can you fill these book boards up with? Try pinning photos and content related to all of the places, people and events that are mentioned within each book. This works great for connecting common themes that appear in your writing and adds an innovative viewing experience for fans and readers.

Hold a Pinterest contest and reward your readers! Ask your readers and fans to submit photos of themselves with your book in random locations, and pin them to your book boards or to an exclusive contest board.

Create a promo pinboard where you collect all your freebie offerings and book launch materials. Remember to include some pins from the press and media coverage your book receives here too, as well as some video content from author interviews!

Create a pinboard of reading recommendations within your genre or compile a list of books you think your readers would also enjoy. Another angle for this approach is to create a pinboard of similar authors or other writers who your style has been compared to.

LinkedIn Promotion for Authors

LinkedIn is the largest social network for professionals, making it a more serious atmosphere than many other social sites. Keep in mind that the LinkedIn crowd are more serious folks and they use the site to network among other professionals in their industry. But don't let that bum you out just yet. When you think about it, that kind of sets the perfect marketing stage for someone who is looking to brand themselves as a published author!

Similar to Facebook, LinkedIn offers a groups feature and you should use it in much the same way when it comes to marketing and promoting your books. Be sure to also keep in mind the etiquette we talked about in the chapter about forum marketing. The same type of rules apply here, so stick to them!

While LinkedIn has many of the standard features found on other social sites, like profiles and status updates (feel free to use these like you do on Facebook and Twitter), it also has a couple of unique features which you can use to market your books as well. The first is Reading List application by Amazon. This is a neat app you can add to your profile which lets your connections see which books you are currently reading. Use this to subtly promote your titles.

When filling out your profile on LinkedIn, pay special attention to the "Publications" section. This is an awesome new way to feature all of your published titles right from within your profile! The coolest thing about this is that you can add any titles you want, even ebooks you wrote and sold or gave away for free on your own website. They don't have to be an Amazon Kindle book or have an ISBN or anything. You can take full advantage of this by including all of your high quality works in this section, including your Kindle books. This adds an extra nod of credibility and works nicely to establish yourself as an expert in your niche.

This may seem like an obvious note, but non-fiction writers and authors probably have a better chance of successfully marketing and promoting their books through LinkedIn. You're not likely to find tons of fiction readers browsing around this site, and even the ones who use the site are probably not going to find their book recommendations from LinkedIn. That's not to say you shouldn't list your fiction books in your profile, but your marketing efforts may be best saved for other social sites that lend to your creativity more, like Pinterest or Twitter.

Google+ Promotion for Authors

While Google's social media effort may not match the likes of Facebook, it does help increase your visibility in Google's search engine, which is obviously pretty important and worth adding to your arsenal of promotion methods for your book.

Here are some basic technical tips for getting started on Google+ if you don't already have a presence on there.

First thing you should do after setting up your Google+ account is make sure that the settings are allowing you search visibility. In this section of your settings, choose the option that says "Help others find my profile in search results."

Customize your profile URL from the default. Use the same ending for your URL as your Twitter username, if the URL is available. Otherwise pick something else that sticks to your overall author brand, but remember to keep it simple and as short as possible. This makes it much easier to remember and share.

Get the image sizes right. Be sure to include the same photos that you commonly use on other social sites, to reinforce your branding efforts. Google+ business pages have two options for featuring photos: five small images or a larger banner image similar to Facebook profiles. The first option calls for five images that are 110 x 110 pixels each. The larger single photo should be 940 x 180 pixels.

Think of your Google+ profile and page as your portfolio or resume. You wouldn't leave any fields on that blank, would you? If you were filling out a job application, then you would need to use creativity for any questions that were difficult for you to answer.

When potential customers visit your Google+ page or profile, they may immediately dismiss you if there is little to no information provided in your profile. Instead, tell them you are an author and list your books. Include links to buy the books on Amazon in the links section of your profile too.

Use Google+ circles feature to segment the people in your network on the site. If you write more than one genre, for example, you can easily group the fans of your fiction and create a separate circle to group the fans of your non-fiction.

Be selective about who you add to your circles. Just like on sites such as Twitter, you should avoid falling into the follow-for-following trap. Just because someone adds you doesn't mean you should or need to add them in return. Instead, focus on the users who interact with you and improve the overall Google+ experience.

If you are interested in reaching out to book bloggers (which I recommend you do) then you can use the circles feature to identify bloggers within your genre and start adding them. This makes it easy to start forming relationships with them, offer exclusive content and start booking dates for your upcoming virtual book tour.

Your Amazon Author Profile

Let's take a moment to focus our attention back on Amazon's site for a moment. You are probably getting so wrapped up in all the different methods for promoting and marketing your book across the web that you may have easily overlooked the marketing opportunities presented by Amazon on their own website, of all places!

This is actually one of the most important stops to make when you set out to start marketing and promoting your titles, so let's spend a few minutes becoming familiar with the different ways to optimize your author profile on Amazon before jumping to the next promotion method.

Before we get started, I suppose we should ask an important question: did you even KNOW that Amazon offers all authors a free profile page that is featured on the product page for their books? If not, you're really missing out!

If you don't already know about Amazon author profiles, then head on over to Google and type in "Amazon Author Central." Click the link and follow the instructions for setting up your author central profile.

So what kind of stuff can you include in your author profile on Amazon? The most important elements are included in the list below.

Author Biography & Photo

This is the meat and bones of your profile, obviously. Take the time to select a professional quality head shot to use in your profile for the best author branding effect. Don't pick an amateur looking snapshot you took with your cell phone and uploaded to Facebook to share with your buddies.

This is your image as an author, so be sure that the photo reflects how you want to be perceived.

As for your author biography, you have tons of options here. A note before you dive in: regardless of what type of bio you decide to submit, your profile will display a disclaimer-style notification that informs visitors that the bio text was provided by the author or their representative.

That being said, it's your call whether you want to write your bio in first person or opt for a more objective tone by using third person instead. The latter style will appear more neutral and may give readers the impression that the bio was written by a publicist, rather than by yourself.

Only you can say whether this is a positive or negative, so give it some thought before choosing the style of your bio.

Blog & Social Media Profiles

Your Amazon Author Profile also gives you the option of adding your blog or website's RSS feed. Using this feature will display your most recent blog posts on your profile, leading more traffic to your site and giving your readers another way to follow you online.

Remember the importance of consistent branding and having a presence on social sites and across the web. This is what will turn your readers into your fans, which is the ultimate goal.

After you add your blog, be sure to include your Twitter username so that your recent tweets will also display on your author profile.

Event Dates & Video

If you have decided to use book trailers or scheduled a virtual book tour as part of your marketing and promotion strategy, then you should definitely use your author profile on Amazon to feature both.

If you have booked upcoming tour appearances on different blogs, then add them to your author profile and include as many details as possible.

Custom Author Profile URL

Be sure that you choose a custom URL for your Amazon author profile when you set it up. Don't keep the automatic one that Amazon assigns you. You should use the same name as your Twitter, Facebook and other social profiles uses, if available.

It should look like this:

http://www.amazon.com/Your-Custom-Name/ASIN

Of course, ASIN will be replaced by your actual Amazon Standard Identification Number, which is a series of numbers and letters that identifies your product, which in this case is your book or ebook.

You can also join the "Search Inside the Book" program offered by Amazon as well, so that potential buyers can read an excerpt from your book before deciding to purchase. This can help to keep your refunds to a minimum, as people will have a better idea of what to expect from your book before they buy.

Book Giveaways for Promotion

Believe it or not, book giveaways are a great way to promote your book and yes, even increase sales too. You might be wondering how in the world you can increase sales by giving your book away for free. Why would you do that instead of get paid for those copies? Let's take a look at the two biggest book giveaway opportunities to answer those questions and doubts.

KDP Select Program

Amazon offers a special program called KDP Select for those authors who want to opt-in. This program adds your title to the Kindle Lending Library, which is only accessible to members of Amazon Prime. These members are then allowed to borrow one title from the library per month. There is no due date for returning them either.

To compensate authors for participating in this program, Amazon set aside about 1.4 million dollars for the year of 2013. The amount you will receive is dependent on how many Prime members borrow your title each month, which you can easily keep track of when you login to your Kindle Direct Publishing account to look at your monthly sales numbers.

There is one big requirement for participation, however. You must agree to only sell your book through Amazon for at least ninety days. After this time period is up, you are free to sell and distribute your books elsewhere. But if you are already selling your book for the Nook or as an iBook, then you will need to first remove it from those programs.

Obviously this isn't for everyone. If you are making good sales on other sites as well, then you may want to explore other options and not opt-in for KDP Select. However, if you're really only selling on Kindle, then this could be a good idea to explore.

KDP Select works incredibly well for fiction authors since readers are less keen on the idea of buying from someone they are not familiar with. Due to the sheer volume of sub-quality fiction for sale in the Kindle store, many buyers have grown wary of new authors.

When one person borrows your book and likes it, they could help you out immensely by telling all of their friends who then borrow or possibly even just buy your book (if they aren't Prime members, they will have to buy.). This works great as word of mouth marketing.

If you choose to enroll your title in KDP Select, then you will be able to choose days on which you will offer your book for free to anyone. This is a very powerful promotion tactic if handled properly. Be sure to give yourself some time to spread the word about the free days. There are actually quite a few sites that list upcoming free Kindle books on their site for readers to keep track of new chances to score free reads.

You will want to submit your free kindle days to these sites to maximize your exposure. They are free to use and work great for promoting your giveaway days. Again, these are going to be readers who buy lots of books so it's worth offering yours for free for a day or two. You can manage to pick up tons of new readers and generate tons of new buzz for your book, including word of mouth since people tend to talk about things they like with friends and family.

List of Sites to Notify for KDP Select Free Days

Pixel of Ink

Pixel of Ink located at www.pixelofink.com is highly recommended as one of the best sites in this list of resources. Head on over to the section called "Author's Corner," and use their form to submit the details of your free Kindle promotion. This is a high traffic site, and you should definitely subscribe to their newsletter for tons of great info as well as request to be featured on their site.

Ereader News Today (www.ereadernewstoday.com)

This is another site that features a new book each day, as well as several free Kindle eBooks. Look near the bottom of their homepage for a contact link and get in touch with them about your upcoming promotion.

Books on the Knob (www.blog.booksontheknob.org)

This site requires you to contact them by email in order to notify them of your Kindle free days. Just look for the contact button on their site and send them your book details and dates.

Indie Book List (www.indiebookslist.com)

This one is very simple, just head on over to fill out the form at Indie Book List and they will list your free days within 24 hours of submission!

Authors on the Cheap
(http://www.facebook.com/AontheC)

Authors on the Cheap is a Facebook page that is open to the public. Just visit the page to submit your free days and include the price, rating and the genre in your description. They will probably remove your post if you fail to provide all of these details.

Effective Teaching Solutions
(http://www.facebook.com/effectiveteachingsolutions)

This is another Facebook page that can be used to share your Kindle free days. They only accept posts from authors of young adult books and require you to include the intended age range and a quick book synopsis.

Amazon's Meet the Author Forum

Don't forget about Amazon's Meet the Author Forum, the only place on the site that permits any self-promotion.

Kindle Boards (www.kindleboards.com)

This is an incredibly useful forum that offers some unique features especially for authors. Be sure to check out the Writer's Cafe after you sign up for your free account. The neatest part about this forum is the Book Bazaar, where you are allowed to start an ongoing thread specifically to promote your books.

This is a rare opportunity as far as forum rules go, so jump all over this! Just stick to their rules, which include only posting to the thread once per week or when responding to a reader. Also, read the full forum rules on the site before posting as each forum has their own idea of proper etiquette. This is a great place to advertise your upcoming Kindle free days if you are participating in KDP Select.

eReader IQ (www.ereaderiq.com)

A little tricky to find the right spot on this site, but it's all the way at the bottom of the page and should say contact. Use this link to let the site know about your Kindle free days.

Kindle Daily Nation (www.kindlenationdaily.com)

Add the upcoming free days for your Kindle ebook on this site's tracker for more exposure. Paid sponsorships are offered here starting at a price of $139.

GoodReads Giveaways

If KDP Select doesn't sound like the right option for you, there is another way to use giveaways as a marketing and promotional tool for your books. You need to head on over to GoodReads.com and sign up for an author account. Next, fill out your profile completely and include a head shot of you (ideally the same one you use across all other sites).

Add your titles to your author profile. Link it up with the Amazon info so that people can click through from the profile to your product page on Amazon, so they can purchase if they want.

GoodReads is an amazing site that is filled with opportunities to network with readers and other authors as well. The site is literally crawling with avid book readers, these are people who read as a hobby and are interested in discovering new authors, whether they are big names or not.

Speaking of big names, there are some rather prolific authors who are making use of GoodReads. It's not just for debut authors and small time publishers. For example, Neil Gaiman, famous author of the Sandman comic book series, is an active user on GoodReads. So this site is definitely worth taking seriously.

Okay, so first thing is first. You will need print copies of your book if you want to do a giveaway on GoodReads. They don't allow eBooks for this particular activity, so you will need to find a print-on-demand publisher to order a few copies before you setup your giveaway contest.

If you have published your eBook with Amazon, it's fairly easy to get a print version setup through CreateSpace, which is also owned by Amazon. It shouldn't cost much, and the process is fairly straightforward.

After you have used CreateSpace's tools to setup your book, you need to order a proof copy which will be sent to you in the mail. Remember to edit your book thoroughly before ordering your proof copy, since you want it to be as close to perfect as possible when it arrives.

Read through the entire printed book when it arrives at your house. Take a highlighter and use it to mark any mistakes that you do not want to be included in the final version. When you're done, go make the appropriate corrections to your manuscript and then resubmit it to CreateSpace before ordering the final version.

Once you are satisfied with the way the book has turned out, go ahead and order as many copies as you want to give away. This is totally up to you, so there is no right or wrong number here. If you just want to give away one copy, that's fine. Or if you have the budget and want to give away fifty, that's fine too!

Once you have the books, you can setup your giveaway on GR. You'll be asked to choose a starting and ending date for the contest. Your book must have been published within the past six months in order to be eligible for a giveaway on GR. Assuming that is the case, then go ahead and decide how long to allow entries into the giveaway.

Don't pick a period of time that is too long, as people are likely to forget about it by the time it ends if you do this. Don't make it too short either though, because you want to give people time to see your giveaway listing and have a chance to sign up.

After the giveaway has started, you can return to GR any time to see how many people have signed up to win a copy. It's pretty normal for this number to be upwards of five hundred, at the least. When the giveaway has ended, GR will select the winners. Their selections are somewhat random, but they do say that they try to match the books with readers who are likely to enjoy them based on their reviews and reading habits.

Once they have chosen the winners, they will provide the addresses where the books should be mailed to. You are responsible for mailing each copy to the winner and must update GR once the books have been sent. They are not fond of people who don't follow through, and it is clearly stated that you won't be welcomed back for any future giveaways if you fail to send the winners their copies.

GoodReads is neat because there tends to be a great number of readers who will end up purchasing your book after the contest is over, even if they didn't win a free copy. The reason for this is that the giveaway made them aware of the book and now they are interested in reading it. So they are much more likely to seek it out afterward.

Also, there is a good chance that the winners will share a review on the website as well. This gives you another avenue for generating buzz and tons of GR users have lots of friends on the site as well, meaning that their reviews will act as powerful recommendations if they like your writing. While GR is somewhat dominated by fiction, like the Kindle store, there is still plenty of room for non-fiction writers.

You can also hold more than one giveaway, as long as they are within the first six months following the original publication date. If you are not sure it will go as well as you would like, then you can always give it a test run by just starting with one copy. That requires very little investment and follow through, so there is really nothing to lose and everything to gain.

Marketing With Your Book Cover

This may seem a bit obvious, but it's important and we don't want to leave it out. While publishing on Amazon is blissfully cheap and affordable for an author, no matter their budget, there are a few things that you will need to invest in if you want to succeed and take your work as an author seriously, like it deserves.

One of the bigger investments you should make when you are producing your book is on a professional graphic designer who can make you a quality cover image. If you read a lot of print books, you probably have noticed that the books of certain authors often share a common theme, such as a specific typeface for their name on each cover. This is a subtle form of branding and you should definitely work with your designer to find the right aesthetic elements to represent you and your work.

This is especially important if you choose to write fiction. Most Kindle success stories in the fiction genre have written several ebooks, oftentimes as part of an ongoing series. This is by far the best approach for fiction authors. If you're doing a series, be sure to tell your designer and talk with them about how you would like for all of the book covers to share some common design accents, and get their advice on what works best.

Other ways to subtly promote your book using the book itself include adding the blurb on the back (more of a print thing, but even eBooks in the Kindle store have a text description) and quotes from editorial reviews of your book. Has your book won any awards?

If so, you will want to work some tasteful bragging into your cover design. Ask the designer to add a small medal in the lower corner of the image and tell them the name of the award you won, so that readers can see this when they are browsing through titles.

For the blurb or back cover of your book, you want to try and sum up your story in about three to four short paragraphs, usually no more than four sentences each. Hint at the highlights without giving away any of the details.

This is an art in and of itself. If you need help learning how to do this effectively, just visit a bookstore and start reading the backs of as many books as possible. You will learn tons from studying the styles of other writers and the way they craft teasers for an interesting story. This can work great to hook in potential readers.

You can also include a short author bio in the front pages, with a head shot and a paragraph or two of text that sums you up as an author. Use the same image that you have used everywhere else on the web. This all comes together to create brand awareness.

Perhaps even more obvious than the book cover is the marketing opportunity that lies within the very title itself. This is different for fiction and non-fiction, but the basic principle is similar.

Your main goal should be to appeal to the reader and make them curious, excited, and interested in finding out more. Fiction titles are often only one or two words. These tend to sound ominous and make people instantly curious because they want to know how the word fits into the story that the book promises to tell. Other fiction titles are several words or sometimes what sounds like even a full sentence. These are far more descriptive and usually give a better idea of what to expect.

Non-fiction is a bit different. With non-fiction, you should think of your book title as being much like your press release headline. It should be very descriptive and each word needs to pack a full punch to really speak to the reader. Remember that the competition is fierce and there are probably tons of other non-fiction books about the same stuff that you are writing about, so you need to set yourself apart from all the noise.

Promote and Market Your Own Website

If you don't already have a website, then it's time to register a domain (preferably your name, but if that's taken then you could try one of your book titles or something close). As a newly published author, you must have a website and you should also be blogging regularly.

Your website is where people will go to find out more about you and your books. This is crucial, so don't put it off or ignore this. You should feature all of your books on the site, and include a synopsis for each of them as well as reviews they have received.

Create one entire page of your site that is completely devoted to your press and media coverage as an author. This is the place you will be uploading all of those mp3 interviews from radio shows and podcasts, so that readers and fans can listen in to learn more about who you are and what you are all about.

Essentially, you will be putting together a press kit for the future. This makes it easier for journalists, reporters, producers and hosts to find you and get a feel for what kind of guest you would make if they decided to contact you with an invitation. And yes, this does happen if you execute all of these marketing strategies correctly. You need to nail it, but when you do, you will know it. They will start coming to you after you've been featured on a few spots here and there.

There are some pretty standard things that should be included in your press kit, let's go through the list briefly:

Author bio (think of your Amazon Author Profile, you can use the same one)

Book synopsis (this goes without saying and each book should have one)

Recent reviews of your book

Author photos

Awards that your books have won

High-quality book cover images

Contact information (address, phone number, email address, make it easy for anyone interested in speaking with you to reach out and become acquainted)

Those are the most basic. But if you really want to setup your press kit in a way that optimizes your desirability for the media, then you should consider trying a few of these extra ideas...

Write down a list of topics that you are well versed in and can speak comfortably about. Basically, tell them what your area of expertise happens to be and provide a few talking points so they can figure out if you are the right type of guest for their show.

To take that idea a step further, include a sample Q&A to paint a clearer picture of what they can expect from you. This could be a transcription of one of your past interviews, or you could make up an example of your own if you prefer. Just give them concrete examples of appropriate questions to ask you and what you are likely to respond with.

Remember, this is your own personal hub for all the publicity you have landed as an author. That means it's okay to include EVERYTHING about you and your books here, that's what this space is made for. This is your own site and people will expect to find this information about you and your books here.

This is also another opportunity to make use of your promotion and marketing tools such as book trailers, virtual book tour dates, interviews, guest blog posts, press releases and anything else you have used as part of your strategy.

Lead Generating Squeeze Page

Okay, so we've covered quite a few methods of promoting your Kindle books, but another important piece to fit into your marketing is a squeeze page that will capture your leads. This form of marketing and promoting may be more familiar territory for seasoned internet marketers, but don't doubt their effectiveness when it comes to building your brand as an author as well.

For example, take a quick look at this squeeze page for the book "No Bullshit Social Media" located at www.nobullshitsocialmedia.com/buythisbook

This page is perfect and it includes all of the most important elements for a book marketing campaign. Notice that "Buy This Book" is prominently displayed where everyone is likely to see it. It jumps out from the page.

Also take note of how the page offers a free chapter for interested visitors to download and sample from the book. This is crucial. You shouldn't expect new readers to trust you or the quality of your work. You have to prove it. Letting them get a taste of what you have to offer is the best way to accomplish this.

So what about fiction books? Should squeeze pages for fiction be the same as those that promote non-fiction? Not quite, though the fundamental concepts should be found on any squeeze page aimed at promoting a book.

For example, let's check out popular Kindle author John Locke's website located at www.donovancreed.com. Mr. Locke has sold over 5 million copies of his ebooks and is one of the hugest self-publishing success stories to date. He writes fiction novels, so his site is a bit more personal.

This is a common theme for fiction authors. They tend to have blogs and oftentimes devote an entire page (linked to in the main navigation menu) for their most popular characters featured in their novels. In the case of John Locke's site, we can see that his main character, Donovan Creed, has a page devoted to all of the novels which include this persona.

There are several more characters featured in Locke's navigation, and the reason for that is the fact that Mr. Locke has published several fiction novels which belong to a series. Clicking on a character name will take you to a list of all titles within that series.

This is something we've talked about before, but it bears repeating. If you are going to tackle the fiction realm, then you almost MUST try to break up your idea into an installment of several books if you want to maximize your success on Kindle. The reason we say this is that nearly EVERY fiction author who has achieved unprecedented success with Kindle has written at LEAST one fiction series.

As a final example for squeeze pages, bestselling author J.A. Konrath has an excellent website located at http://www.jakonrath.com and blog where he features his titles and categorizes them by the series they belong to, similar to Locke's website. He also actively blogs and shares info with his visitors and readers by offering email newsletters and updates.

A really neat added feature on Konrath's site is his "Store," link from the navigation menu along the left side. When you click on it, you will be taken to a page where you can order print copies of his books directly from the author himself. He has used Paypal buttons for accepting payment and offers to send buyers signed copies as well.

This is a nice personal touch, but may not make sense for someone just starting out. If you order copies from a print-on-demand publisher (like Creatspace, owned by Amazon) then you might consider setting up a store on your site to sell any leftover copies. Once you've built a fan base, as Konrath has, then you may even have fans who are after a signed copy from you as well. Dream big.

So as we can see, there are some things which just about every squeeze page for a book should include. Those are: a free chapter sample, newsletter or blog, cover image, synopsis, bio/about me, links to purchase the book on various sites, reviews, media coverage and author interviews. Video may be considered a potentially essential aspect of a squeeze page as well.

Use these examples to model your own page once you get started on creating your book launch campaign.

Understanding and Mastering the Amazon Kindle Book Ecosystem

The scientific definition of an ecosystem is a community of living and non-living things that work together. When I refer to the Amazon Kindle book ecosystem I'm referring to everything on the Amazon site that work together and affect the positioning, marketing and selling of your Kindle book in the Amazon Kindle store. Things like your book's website, blog, video trailer, and social media accounts like Facebook, Twitter etc. are everything that happens outside of the Amazon Kindle book ecosystem.

So why must you understand and master the variables that make up the Amazon Kindle book ecosystem? Because understanding and mastering the various variables are essential for your Kindle book's success. These different variables serve as indicators to Amazon whether or not your Kindle book is generating interest and activity. If your Kindle book is generating interest and activity Amazon will further promote it and vice versa.

I know that you are probably wondering how does Amazon know if your book is generating interest or activity? Well the answer is they look at the metrics. Metrics are simply a measurement of activity and performance. Examples of metrics that Amazon would use to measure your book's activity and performance are:

- The total amount of visitors to your Kindle book's product page.
- The total amount of "likes" your Kindle book has received.
- The total amount of customer reviews.

- The average rating of those customer reviews
- The amount of relevant tags your Kindle book has.
- The total amount of sales.
- The frequency of those sales.
- The total amount of "free" downloads.
- How many times people bought your Kindle book after it being recommended by Amazon. For example "Customers Who Bought This Item Also Bought".
- Your sales rank in comparison to other similar books in the same genre.
- The refund rate.

I mean just think about it logically for a moment, what other criteria could they possibly use as a measurement to determine activity or interest? Now that you have a clear picture of the point that I'm trying to drive home let's discuss these variables and components that make up and heavily influence the Amazon Kindle book ecosystem.

Activity

Based on my experience, I have determined that when your Kindle book becomes available on Amazon it's best to have a lot of activity going on. One thing that you can do to immediately stimulate activity is by offering your Kindle book as a free download.

As mentioned earlier, to offer your Kindle book as a free download you have to enroll it in the KDP Select program. If you want to get the maximum amount of downloads offer your book for free for 5 consecutive days. Remember your purpose for doing this is to generate massive activity and get your Kindle book percolating in the Amazon Kindle book ecosystem.

If your book's genre is a hot one in terms of interest and you have crafted the title of your book so that it stands out and arouses curiosity and you have created both a killer cover and description of your book, you should get a great deal of free downloads.

Once your book begins to get downloads and crosses a certain threshold, it begins to get ranked in the free Kindle store as well as in the categories that you've chose when uploading your book and the categories that Amazon arbitrarily assigns.

Your goal at this point should be to make the top 100 best sellers list in your book's category. For example, if you have a Kindle book listed in the business and investing category you at least want to make the top 100 free best sellers list. Preferably and ideally you want to get your Kindle book ranked somewhere in the top 10 position of this particular list.

That's why it is extremely important that you get the word out as much as possible about your free download dates as this will help you reach the top of the free best sellers list in your book's category.

A lot of Kindle book authors usually balk at the idea of giving their Kindle book away for free and a great deal of them don't and this where they err in judgment. They don't realize or understand the Kindle book ecosystem and how you actually get rewarded by Amazon by contributing to it in the form offering free downloads.

Let me explain. Amazon sells a ton of Kindle devices therefore they need content for the customers who have bought these e-readers. Of course these customers can purchase their Kindle books and they do however, to keep customers engaged and addicted to the Kindle experience Amazon makes available to them the opportunity to download Kindle books for free.

This serves several purposes, it gives the customers the opportunity to discover books they would of have never read and sample new authors they would have never given a chance because they simply never heard of them or they weren't promoted in the mainstream media.

If they have had a positive experience from the free download, it is Amazon's hope that this will instill the confidence in them to eventually make paid purchases even if the author or book is unknown to them.

Now the way Amazon rewards you for allowing your Kindle book to be downloaded for free is by giving your book more exposure. Your Kindle book starts appearing all over the Kindle book ecosystem. Even though your Kindle book was downloaded for free, Amazon counts it as a sale in their system.

I know that this sounds odd but it's the truth. Your Kindle book will start appearing in recommendations like "Customers Who Bought This Item Also Bought", "What Other Items Do Customers Buy After Viewing This Item?" or "More Items To Consider".

This is a brilliant marketing tactic by Amazon and your Kindle book benefits immensely by increased exposure which will result in more paid sales. Speaking of sales, usually after your Kindle "free" download period is over, you will see a bump in sales.

Another thing that Amazon does once your book shows activity in their Kindle book ecosystem is they will send out emails promoting your Kindle book as well as others to customers who have shown interest in your book's subject matter or genre. The way that Amazon determines what customers might be interested in possibly purchasing your book or other books on the subject matter is either by their past purchases of similar books or based on their browsing history.

For example, I downloaded for free a Kindle book in the money and banking genre on the subject matter of hedge funds. A few weeks later I received an email from Amazon. That email had the following heading in the subject line: **Money & Markets: Top Investment Banking Guides**. Now of course that piqued my interest so needless to say I opened the email.

When I opened the email it contained 6 Kindle books on the topic of hedge funds. Since I was interested in learning more about hedge funds I browsed to each and every one of those books and used the "look inside" feature to sample the content. Once I was satisfied with the sample content I made a purchase. This segues right into another important variable that will strongly determine whether or not you get sales for your Kindle book: the "Look Inside" feature.

"Look Inside" Feature

The "Look Inside" feature for Kindle books on Amazon allows potential customers to sample your book to determine whether or not they want to buy it. They are allowed to sample the first 10% of your book. They can access the "Look Inside" feature directly on Amazon's website or they can have their free sample delivered to them wirelessly to their e-reader of choice whether that's the Kindle, the Ipad or whatever e-reader application they are utilizing.

The first 10% of your book will either get you the sale or lose you the sale so it is extremely important that the content in the beginning of your book is persuasive enough to convert your book's prospects into customers. You must remember that since your potential customers only get a 10% sample of the beginning of your book it is imperative that they are able to get to the main writing immediately.

If you have such things as copyright information, legal notices, tributes, dedications etc. in your book you don't want them to be long winded, because they count towards that first 10%. It's not like any of those things will clinch the sale anyway. If you eliminate some of these things so that your prospect can sample more of your actual book the better.

That's why for example in the Kindle version of this particular book the first thing the potential customer sees when they access the "look inside" feature is the cover which is followed by the table of contents ,which is then followed by the introduction and after the introduction they get a chance to read more content of substance.

I have structured it in a way that when the prospect reads the first 10% of my book, it should clinch the sale if they are truly interested in learning pertinent marketing tactics and strategies that will enable them to sell more Kindle books.

So my advice to you is that you should spend some extra time crafting and reviewing the first 10 % of your book because it is a big determining factor in whether you get the sale or not. You should make sure that it contains substance, is devoid of fluff and has an adequate amount of emotional and persuasive triggers that will lead to the sale.

Also of equal importance is your book cover which I covered earlier. People judge a book by its cover and if your cover is not up to par or doesn't look professionally done, why would someone be stimulated, persuaded, or inspired to "Look Inside" your Kindle book? Your Kindle book cover is the first impression that the browser will get of your book, so you must make certain that it is impressive, stands out, is designed well and the title of your book is easy to decipher.

Tags

Tags are another important variable in the Amazon Kindle book ecosystem because they help readers find your book more easily. A tag is simply a keyword or category label strongly related to a product. For example, some of the tags that can be associated with this book are:

- Kindle book marketing
- Kindle book promotion
- How to sell Kindle books
- Ebook sales
- Kindle publishing
- Tips for Kindle authors

Tags are also part of Amazon's secret recipe that they use to determine in what order books will appear when a search is performed. The more your Kindle book is tagged with relevant keywords the more people will be able to find your book and the more people are able to find your book, the more books you will sell.

I know that sales are also a big part of this secret recipe, but the importance of tags should not be ignored. So how do you get tags for your Kindle book? Well the first step would be for you to create your own book tags.

In order to for you to tag your book on Amazon and have other people be able to see those tags, you need to have an account on Amazon and have a history of at least one purchase. If you tag your Kindle book and you have never purchased anything on Amazon, your tags will be only visible to you and wont aid in increasing your book's popularity.

To increase your tag count you should ask your family, friends, and associates etc. to also tag your book, of course right after they have purchased it. It is important to tell them that when they tag your book they should make sure they are doing so with relevant keywords and search terms that people are more apt to use when looking for books in your book's genre. Please be aware that each person can tag your book up to 15 times because that is the maximum amount of tags Amazon allows each person.

As your book gets tagged you will notice that there is a number next to those tags. Those numbers indicate how many people also tagged your book using the same tags. Why are the total amount of tags your book gets on each keyword so important? Because tags are clickable and when you click on them they lead you directly to a community. In this community the products with the most tags will be displayed front and center for that community.

For example, say for instance someone is looking at tags on another book that's similar to yours and they clicked on a popular tag that is identifiable with what they are searching for. If your book has more tags than that particular book as well as other competitors, your potential customer will see your book at the top of the list in that community. This visibility and positioning will enable you to sell a lot more Kindle books.

"Likes"

Amazon has a "like" button similar to the one that we've grown accustomed to seeing on Facebook. Amazon utilizes the "like" button to fine tune the recommendations that it makes to its customers. If you click on the "like" button on the product page of a particular book, shortly thereafter you will start to see recommendations of other similar books in the "recommended" section of your Amazon account.

Although Amazon primarily uses the "like" button to find out more about their customers, for book marketing purposes it can be utilized as an indication of social acceptance similar to the "like" buttons on Facebook and YouTube. When people see that a book has a good amount of "likes", they tend to be more persuaded to make a purchase.

I know that you are probably thinking "why would people "like" my book and they probably haven't read it?" Well, in some cases they might have read it then went back on Amazon to leave a review and while they were there they probably felt inspired to also click on the "like" button. Or maybe they read a sample of your book using the "Look Inside" feature or they had a sample delivered wirelessly to their e-reader and after they read the sample they went on Amazon and clicked on the "like" button.

The bottom line is, getting "likes" are important and you should try to get as many as you possibly can legitimately because they make your book look attractive to others. To get "likes", once again you can ask family, friends or associates to do the honors for you when they go to buy your book.

Price and Royalty Rate

The way you price your Kindle book determines what royalty rate Amazon pays you and it also determines how well your book sells.

First, let's tackle royalty rates. You get a 70% royalty rate from Amazon when you price your book between $2.99 and $9.99. However, as of this writing the 70% royalty option only applies to the following the countries:

Andorra

Austria

Belgium

Brazil*

Canada

France

Germany

India*

Italy

Japan*

Liechtenstein

Luxembourg

Monaco

San Marino

Switzerland

Spain

United Kingdom (including Guernsey, Jersey and Isle of Man)

United States

Vatican City

To receive a 70% royalty rate from the countries with asterisk next to them (Brazil, Japan and India) you have to be enrolled in the KDP Select program and if you're not enrolled you will receive a 35% royalty rate for Kindle books sold in those respective countries. A 35% royalty rate is also paid for Kindle books priced below $2.99 regardless of the country.

Why do you think Amazon pays a royalty rate of 70% for Kindle books priced between $2.99 and $9.99? It is because they know what their "sweet spot" is in terms of what price range generates the most sales for them.

Also it is their overall goal as a company to deliver the best value to the customer at the lowest possible price. How do I know this? I heard it directly from Amazon's CEO Jeff Bezos mouth on the Charlie Rose television show. That's why they make sure that you rarely see Kindle books priced above $9.99 because if you price your Kindle book above that you won't be eligible for the 70% royalty pay out.

I must also note that in the calculation of your royalty payment delivery costs are factored in. I know you are probably thinking "what delivery cost? Aren't Kindle books delivered digitally?" Yes they are but Amazon has managed to factor in delivery cost based on the amount of megabytes your book contains. This delivery cost usually amounts to around .02 cents.

So the actual formula for calculating a 70% royalty payment if you sold a Kindle book in the United Kingdom would be:

Royalty Rate X (List Price - Delivery Costs) = Royalty

Kindle Book Pricing Strategies

Ok now let's discuss pricing your Kindle book. When it comes to this topic most Kindle book authors or publishers are always searching for the ideal price in which to sell their Kindle books. Should they price their books at $2.99, $3.99, $4.99 or .99 cents? The answer is it all depends on what you are trying to accomplish with your Kindle book and what the market will bear.

For example, say you wrote your Kindle book specifically for lead generation. Although obviously you want to make money from the sale of your Kindle book this may not be your main objective, getting leads are because maybe you are offering something on the backend at a higher price that will more than compensate for the low pricing of your Kindle book.

Kindle books that are priced for lead generation are usually short ,contains a powerful burst of valuable information , and have a strong "call to action" that is designed to get the reader to do something specifically like subscribe to a newsletter, visit a website etc. Lead generation Kindle books are typically priced between $.99 and $2.99.

Kindle book buyers show little resistance to books priced in this range so they usually gobble them up without hesitation. For example, I presently have 5 amazing Kindle books that I use as a source for lead generation. These books are priced at .99 cents and they contain an incredible amount of valuable information. They are as follows:

- How To Make Money Online: The Savvy Entrepreneur Guide To Financial Freedom

- How To Create A Profitable Ezine From Scratch

- How To Make A Fortune Using The Public Domain

- How To Overcome Your Self Limiting Beliefs

- The Secrets Of Finding The Perfect Ghostwriter For Your Book

Don't misunderstand me you can price your Kindle book if it is designed for lead generation at a much higher price range than .99 cents to $2.99 as this is not etched in stone. I suggest that you test different price ranges to see which one yields the optimum results for you in terms of sales, profits and response rate.

Amazon makes this fairly easy for you, by allowing you to change the price of your Kindle books anytime you want. Once you've changed your price it usually takes up to 24 hours to show up on Amazon.

Now in regards to fiction Kindle books, I've seen them priced as low as .99 cents and priced all the way up to $14.99. The fiction Kindle books that are priced higher than $9.99 are usually from well-known authors such as John Grisham or Nora Roberts.

Nonetheless, the price that you assign to your Kindle book is of utmost importance to your book's success. If you price your book too high, the marketplace will let you know because you will receive few book sales or possibly none at all. If you price it too low, you could be devaluing your own content plus sometimes when people see a book at a very cheap price they may assume that it doesn't have valuable content so they don't buy it.

If you want to create a self-sustaining business strictly from the sales of your Kindle books then profit will be the main determining factor in how you price your books. Let me give you a vivid example of how price affects how much money you make.

There's a big difference between selling 500 Kindle books at $6.99 versus selling 500 Kindle books at .99 cents. If you sell 500 Kindle books at $6.99 you are entitled to the 70% royalty rate so you would get $4.89 per book sold which is (70% X $6.99 = $4.89) without taking into account the delivery costs which we must factor in.

Let's say the delivery costs are .02 per book, the total delivery costs would be $10 which is (500 X .02 cents = $10). Your net profit would be a total of $2,435 which is calculated the following way (500 X $4.89 minus $10 = $2,435). Pretty good right?

Now let's look at the numbers if the list price of those same 500 Kindle books were .99 cents each. At .99 cents your royalty rate would be 35%, so you would get .35 cents for every book sold. In this case that equals 500, so you would make a total of $175 which is simply calculated the following way (500 X .35 =$175). Tell me if your goal is to have a self sustaining Kindle book business what would you rather make $2,435 or $175?

$2,435 can pay a mortgage payment or rent and depending where you live you might even have enough left over to make a car payment. While all $175 would probably get you is a nice dinner and possibly a movie with your significant other.

Don't get me wrong there are always exceptions to the rule. For example, best selling Kindle book author John Locke initially priced his novels at .99 cents and as a result has managed to sell over 1 million Kindle books in just 5 months.

Although lately I've seen an increase in his prices for some of his Kindle books (they now hover around the $2.99 price range) nonetheless, he used the .99 cent pricing format to catapult himself to Kindle book author super stardom by becoming only the second independent author to sell 1 million books through the Kindle publishing platform.

The lesson to be learned from John Locke and can be adopted as a pricing strategy is to start off your Kindle books at a lower price (maybe not .99 cents), so that you can move a great deal of them fast and in volume, then once you have obtained a certain amount of sales you bump your prices up. Like I've mentioned before nothing is etched in stone in regards to the strategy that you would use to price your books, so be flexible.

In concluding this topic on pricing strategies, if you are producing some sort of specialty Kindle book that is niche oriented and is on a highly technical topic where quality information is extremely hard to find, you can price your book at the higher end of the totem pole.

Examples of this type of specialty book would be a text book or a book on PHP or MySQL web development. Speaking on the latter, I actually purchased a Kindle book on PHP and MySQL web development for $25.

The Description of Your Kindle Book

The description details of your Kindle book on your Amazon product page will either make or break you in terms of sales. Your book's description in most cases is what people will read to determine whether or not they want to buy your book or read a sample of it before deciding to buy it or not.

Unfortunately, I see a lot of Kindle book publishers mangle this important component of the Kindle book ecosystem by mistakenly viewing the description area as simply a place where you summarize your book. The truth of the matter is your book's description is actually your sales copy. It's there to sell your book, so you must make sure that it absolutely does.

Remember, chances are your book is up against some stiff competition with other Kindle books in its genre so it is imperative that in your description you convey what makes your book uniquely different from the others.

Your Unique Selling Position

This positioning is referred to as your unique selling position. Your unique selling position if crafted and expressed properly can skyrocket your Kindle book sales. If you were creating a unique selling position for a non-fiction book, you would simply analyze your book's content to determine what makes it uniquely different from other books that are also covering the same topic or subject matter.

Once you figure out what makes your book special and what motivates your target audience, you have found your unique selling position and you need to highlight and emphasize it.

Another important element that will also help you close the sale are the benefits that the reader will get as a result of purchasing and reading your non-fiction Kindle book. Does your book help to solve a particular problem? If so that's a benefit and you should include it in the description. Will the reader get some type of pleasure or excitement from reading your book? If so that is another benefit that you can also highlight in your book's description.

How To Write A Killer Description For Your Non-Fiction Kindle Book

Here is a check list that you can use and some questions you need to ask yourself before deciding on your non-fiction book's description:

- Does it grab the reader's attention quickly as possible?
- Does it make an emotional connection?
- Does it identify the problems that the reader wants to solve?
- Does the description indicate that your book offers the solution to these particular problems?
- Are the benefits stated?
- Does it include testimonials?
- Did you remember to sell the sizzle and not the steak?

How To Write A Killer Description For Your Fiction Kindle Book

Writing a description for fiction books is somewhat different than writing a description for a non-fiction book. The words that you would use to describe a fiction novel depends on what type of book it is.

For example, words that could be potentially associated with a thriller would be **creepy, scary, suspenseful, horrifying,**

terrifying, pulse pounding. Words that can be use to describe a romance novel would be **heart-warming, uplifting, heartfelt, heartbreaking, tear-jerking, romantic, steamy**.

While we are on the subject of descriptive words for fiction books here is a list of 27 vivid words that you can use to describe your Kindle book:

- action-packed
- addictive
- adventurous
- amusing
- astonishing
- awe-inspiring
- believable
- breath-taking
- brilliant
- charismatic
- charming
- comforting
- complex
- complicated
- engaging
- entertaining
- exciting
- exhilarating
- fanciful
- fascinating
- gripping
- inspirational
- mysterious
- mystical

- powerful
- page-turner
- riveting

Ok now let's go over the important elements that will enable you to create a killer description for your fiction book.

You must have a powerful strapline. A strapline is usually the first line in your book's description and if you don't get the first line right people won't read the rest of your description. So it is important that you make sure that your strapline not only encapsulates your entire book but also is powerful enough to draw people in.

For example here is the strapline in the description from the book The Racketeer by best-selling author John Grisham.

"Given the importance of what they do, and the controversies that often surround them, and the violent people they sometimes confront, it is remarkable that in the history of this country only four active federal judges have been murdered."

"Judge Raymond Fawcett has just become number five."

This strapline immediately tells the reader what kind of book this is. It's obviously a legal thriller and you are immediately drawn in to read the rest of the description because the strapline compels you to by adding intrigue, mystery and suspense. This is exemplified by the following text in the strapline:

"It is remarkable that in the history of this country only four active federal judges have been murdered. Judge Raymond Fawcett has just become number five."

I'm interested in reading on in the description to perhaps get some sort of clue why Judge Raymond Fawcett has just become the 5th judge murdered and of course I'm only given a small dose of clues in the description. To find out more about the circumstances surrounding the death of Judge Raymond Fawcett, I have to buy the book.

You must bring your characters alive. After the strapline comes the body of your description and this is where you must bring the characters of your story alive. It is important that people emotionally connect with your characters. To accomplish this you would describe your characters emotional make up, personality and the big problem they are facing or dealing with without giving away the story.

For example, the description of the book Addicted To My Sugar by Mack Collins the main character of the story "Liz" is described the following way to breathe life into her and to also get the reader to make an emotional connection:

"Juggling, school, rent and bills seems like all too much for Liz. Her dream car is just that, a DREAM! Why did her life have to be so, so hard? Her job on campus does not help the situation much either. What is she to do?

Should she find herself a man who provides money or other favors in exchange for sexual relations to ease her burdens? Should she go get herself a Sugar Daddy that will spoil her rotten?"

You must conclude your description with a resounding cliff hanger. The end of your description is the last chance that you have to convince the browser and potential customer to buy your book so it must be effective. To make it as effective as possible I strongly suggest that you end it with a cliff hanger, something that leaves them on the edge of their seats wanting more! It should be a hint of something more exciting to come. Something that inspires or convinces them to buy your book right now!

For example, here is John Grisham's cliff hanger in the description of his book The Racketeer:

What was in the safe? The FBI would love to know. And Malcolm Bannister would love to tell them. But everything has a price—especially information as explosive as the sequence of events that led to Judge Fawcett's death. And the Racketeer wasn't born yesterday.

This cliff hanger is a doozy and of course it inspires the reader to make a purchase to find out more.

The Importance of Copywriting

To understand how your sales copy for your book should be written you need to know a little bit about copywriting. Copywriting is the art and science of strategically using words to persuade your intended target to take action which in your case is the purchase of your Kindle book.

Copywriting is formulaic in nature and its elements consist of a headline, a subhead, body copy, bulleted points, testimonials, "a call to action" and other important elements. Traditional publishers or prominent authors usually hire professional copywriters to create persuasive sales copy for their books.

Of course you don't need to do that, you only need to have a simple understanding of the basic principles of copywriting so that you can effectively write your own sales copy. To assist you with that I've created a Kindle book entitled "**How To**

Sell Any Product Online: "Secrets of The Killer Sales Letter" that will have you up to speed in no time.

How To Make Your Description Stand Out Using HTML Coding

As I mentioned already copywriting is formulaic in nature and this formula includes the way in which your words are laid out in the description area of your Kindle book's web page. The way your description is laid out is of utmost importance because when most people read they usually scan what's written and this includes your potential customer.

They look for things that stand out on the page like headings, bold and italicized words, bulleted points etc. To obtain the aforementioned desired effects you must use html coding. Don't be alarmed, it's all quite simple. Let me give you a quick lesson on the html coding that Amazon specifically uses on its website. Look at the coding below and to achieve the desired effect you would insert your text where it says "Your Text".

H1 Headline (The is the largest font size that Amazon allows)

<h1>YOUR TEXT</h1>

H2 HEADING (Amazon Orange)

<h2>YOUR TEXT</h2>

HEADLINE AND CENTERED

<center><h2>YOUR TEXT</h2></center>

NUMBERED LIST

<ol>

<li>YOUR TEXT</li>

<li>YOUR TEXT</li>

<li>YOUR TEXT</li>

</ol>

BULLETED LIST

<ul>

<li>YOUR TEXT</li>

<li>YOUR TEXT</li>

<li>YOUR TEXT</li>

</ul>

UNDERLINED

<u>YOUR TEXT</u>

BOLD

<b>YOUR TEXT</b>

ITALICS

<i>YOUR TEXT</i>

CENTERED

<center>YOUR TEXT</center>

This whole coding thing may seem a bit confusing to you so if you don't want to beat yourself over the head learning Amazon's html coding you can simply outsource the task. There are a few great coders on Fiverr.com that would be more than happy to perform this task for you for a measly $5. All you would have to do is go to Fiverr.com and in their search engine perform a search using the keyword term "Amazon html code" and you will be able to locate people who will be able to do the job for you.

In closing this particular topic on your book's description, please note that Amazon only allows you to use 4,000 characters in the description area so it is essential that you make every word count.

Customer Reviews

Reviews are very important to your Kindle book's success. Here's why. They serve as social proof that others positively or negatively get influenced by. Social proof is a psychological phenomenon where people assume the actions of others in an attempt to reflect the correct behavior for a given situation. Simplifying it even further, social proof is based on a herd mentality and the majority of people are wired to follow the herd.

When we witness others doing something, we automatically and subconsciously determine that it is safe and even in our best interest to do the same. For example, when we see money in the tip jar we are subconsciously and consciously influenced to leave a tip because the evidence strongly suggests that others have done so.

That's why the person who is in charge of the tip jar always puts money in it before placing it strategically in plain view on the counter because he or she knows that a tip jar with money already in it will strongly influence people to tip.

Book reviews work the same way, they influence people to buy or not to buy. If a book has great reviews people are more apt to purchase it and if it has a great deal of negative reviews the opposite effect occurs.

Now am I saying that your Kindle book needs to have all 5 star reviews to sell? I'm not saying that at all in fact, let's say you had 25 reviews for your Kindle book and all 25 reviews had 5 stars, people will become somewhat skeptical. It's the nature of the beast.

They will think that those reviews were planted by you the author. Five star reviews are great especially if they are well deserved but keep in mind it's good to also have some thorough critical reviews.

When I refer to thorough critical reviews I'm talking about reviews with 3 or 4 stars that have a thorough explanation as to why they were rated that way. For example, here's a 4 star critical review of Addicted To My Sugar Daddy by author Mack Collins who is signed to my publishing umbrella Make Profits Easy LLC.

"Anyone ever wonder what it would be like if they had a sugar daddy, well here you go. I don't know about you but I thought about it a time or two(not seriously though). Here we have Liz, struggling to make ends meet while going to college. Her friend, Suzie suggests she try a sugar daddy then all her troubles will just go away.

That's where all her troubles begin, she ends up juggling three guys. My first impression of these three guys were that I didn't like Joey at first, I liked Mike and Alec, to be honest wasn't in the book long enough to make an impression.

This book was a quick, hot, read. I enjoyed this book, for all its hotness as well as its storyline. Even though I was surprised at the ending, the author tied up the story pretty neatly.

Warning, if you don't like a lot of sexual situations in your books then this isn't for you. But if you are looking for just a hot read with a good story behind it then give this book a try.

I received complimentary copy of the book in exchange for an honest review."

I consider this to be a great critical 4 star review because the reviewer liked the book but in her opinion she didn't think that one of main characters Alec was in the book long enough to make an impression on her. She was also upfront because at the end of the review she let people know that she received a "complimentary copy of the book in exchange for an honest review."

The Secret To Getting Trusted Reviews For Your Kindle Book

It is imperative that you get reviews for your Kindle book because the "social proof" will help drive your sales. To start off you can get your family and friends to purchase your Kindle book and give you reviews but eventually you will exhaust that option.

Not only will you exhaust that option, if you are consistently releasing Kindle books to constantly put yourself in the position of asking your family and friends to review your Kindle books will become a drag. A drag to you and a drag to them.

So here is a much more reliable and effective way to get reviews. Not just any ol' reviews but "trusted reviews". So what exactly is a "trusted review"? A "trusted review" is a review that comes from someone that you can expect to give their honest opinion because they have a great history of doing so and they have proven to be authoritative when it comes to giving reviews.

A review from a "trusted reviewer" will hold more weight and social proof than a review from the average Joe or Jane. In fact, if you're able to get a substantial amount of "trusted reviews" for your Kindle book it will impact your Kindle book sales dramatically.

The way that you would find these authoritative and trusted reviewers to review your Kindle book is by searching for them on Amazon. Here's a link that will lead you to the Amazon top ranking reviewers page.

http://www.amazon.com/review/top-reviewers

Here you will find Amazon's community of "trusted reviewers" who are listed according to their rank by Amazon. A lot of these "trusted reviewers" have left reviews on hundreds and even thousands of products on Amazon and as such they are held in high esteem by buyers because they represent strong social proof to whether a product or a book is worthy of being purchased.

There are 10,000 of these "trusted reviewers" listed so how would you find the ones that have given book reviews in your genre? I have discovered the secret way to accomplish this and let me share it with you. Go to Google's search engine and type in the following:

inurl:http://www.amazon.com/gp/pdp/profile

Next, at the end of the aforementioned link in quotations type in a keyword or keyword phrase that is related to your Kindle book's category or niche then click the search button and the results will render a list of profiles of trusted Amazon reviewers that have reviewed books in your Kindle book's category or niche.

For example, if you were in the children's book niche your search parameters would look like this:

inurl:http://www.amazon.com/gp/pdp/profile"children books"

To get your Kindle book reviewed by a particular reviewer all you would have to do is click on their profile link and most of the time it contains their contact information like an email address, website address, or Facebook page. Simply contact them and explain that you are interested in getting your Kindle book reviewed.

Here is an email template that you can use:

Hello (reviewer's name),

I'm author (your name) and I was wondering if you'd be interested in receiving and reviewing my book, (the title of your book).

Here is the blurb:

(Here you would insert a short summary or description of your book)

The genre is (you would put your book's genre). Word count is: (you would put your book's word count).

Here's a link to the awesome cover: (here you would insert the url of your book cover)

Thank you so much for all you do and taking the time to read my email. I hope to hear from you soon!

Sincerely,

(Your Name)

There may be a great deal of Amazon "trusted reviewers" in your Kindle book's genre and emailing each one individually can become quite tedious and time consuming. To alleviate that painstaking and tedious process, I suggest that you use a bulk email sender software to make this task more manageable. The bulk email sender software that I presently use to contact "trusted reviewers" and book bloggers is called Turbo Mailer.

Turbo Mailer is a mass mailer software for preparing and sending bulk email. It is very simple and easy to use and reasonably priced at $9.90. Here are some of the key features:

- Intuitive User Interface, Text & HTML Editor
- Sends bulk HTML & Text Email, Attachments and Embedded Images
- Message personalization
- Imports address lists and personalization columns from local text files, from tables (e.g. Excel, CSV)

As you can clearly see, this is a powerful tool to have in your Kindle book marketing arsenal. For more information on Turbo Mailer visit the following web address:

http://www.xellsoft.com/TurboMailer.html

Most Helpful Customer Reviews

Amazon offers people the chance to vote whether or not a review has been helpful to them. This option is located under each and every review and the question is stated the following way: Was this review helpful to you? Then there is a yes or no button that you can click on that records and tallies your vote. If you are really in the mood you can also leave a comment about the particular review that you are voting on.

Why is this feature so important to the success of your Kindle book? It is very important to your book's success because the more votes a review has the higher it appears on the page. So if someone wrote a not so favorable review of your book and this particular review has more "yes" votes than other reviews, it will appear at the top position and you don't want that to happen simply because that is the first review that your potential customers will see when deciding whether or not to buy your book.

It will actually show a count of how many people voted for that particular review as helpful. For instance it will say: 29 of 29 people found the following review helpful. If your book gets a scathing review and that review is at the top of the page then it is in your best interest to see that particular review get voted down and relegated to the bottom of the page and ideally below the cut-off point.

What I mean by the cut-off point is this. After a book gets a certain amount of reviews Amazon only shows the first couple of reviews (which is the cut-off point) and to see the rest of the reviews that are not shown you must click on a link that says "see all customer reviews". It makes perfect sense for you to want to see your most favorable reviews at the top of the page.

I'm not against people leaving honest reviews because after all they are entitled to their opinions, I just wanted to show you some options so that you will be able to protect yourself against unjustified reviews because if you get one and you contact Amazon about it they won't do anything.

For example, I received a review on one of my Kindle books that was not only unjust but it was blatantly posted as a form of promotion for another author's book in the same genre. They actually included a link back to that author's book in the review. I contacted Amazon about this and the response I got was the following:

"I understand your concerns, but the review doesn't violate our posted guidelines, so I'm unable to remove it in its current format. However, as the author of this title, you can provide feedback about this review by voting or commenting on it. To vote, click the "Yes" or "No" buttons next to "Was this review helpful to you?" To comment, click the Comments link at the bottom of the review."

"We try to encourage our customers to give their honest opinions on our products while staying within our guidelines. As a retailer we are interested in cultivating a diversity of opinion on our products. Part of that is allowing our customers to air their honest thoughts on items they have received."

So as you can clearly see Amazon doesn't care if you as an author vote down a negative review which in this case I most certainly did. Another thing you should pay attention to is that although the reviewer left a link back to another Kindle book in the same genre, Amazon said it didn't violate their policy.

If it doesn't violate their policy, what stops you from using this as a promotion tactic for your own Kindle book? (Wink Wink) It doesn't, I just hope that if you decide to use this as a marketing tactic you don't harm another author's book just so your book can get more attention. That wouldn't be right and karma may come back to haunt you.

Secret Strategy That You Can Use To Easily Get "Amazon Verified Purchase" Reviews

When you get a review you want it to be a review from someone who has purchased your Kindle book because it will show up under the reviewer's name as an "Amazon Verified Purchase". An "Amazon Verified Purchase" review holds more weight from Amazon as well as to the people who are reading it to determine whether or not they are going to buy your book.

While we are on the topic of "Amazon Verified Purchase" reviews here is a legitimately and secret way that you can get them for your Kindle book. All you would have to do to is send your Kindle book as "a gift" and when the person who has received your Kindle book as a gift leaves a review it shows up as an "Amazon Verified Purchase". How cool is that?

And to boot you even get a royalty payment for sending your book as a gift. So let's say that before you sent your Kindle book out as a gift you lowered the price to .99 cents, for every book that you "gift" at .99 cents you will earn.35 cents in royalties (lol).

How To Get More Exposure and Sales For Your Kindle Book By Choosing The Right Categories

Amazon allows you to choose up to two categories for your Kindle book. Most Kindle book authors don't really give too much thought to their decision when choosing their two categories and as a result they receive less exposure and less sales. Choosing the most effective categories for your book is highly important because people use categories to browse and locate books in the niche that they are interested in.

For example, I really love books on entrepreneurship I devour them at such an amazing speed especially the popular ones that I quickly need new titles in which to choose from. So what I do is go to Amazon's main page and click where it says "shop by the department" and I then guide my mouse to where it says "books" and then I click on where it says "Kindle books" and I am taken directly to the Kindle book store where on the side bar of that page I am given a choice of categories to choose from.

The main category that I choose when I am looking for books on entrepreneurship is the Business and Investing category. After clicking on that category I am led to a subcategory of choices which includes the sub category "Small Business and Entrepreneurship".

I click on that sub category and Amazon gives me all the Kindle books that are listed in that category and I am able to sort them by average customer review, publication date, price (low to high and high to low) or by the ones that are new and popular. I usually choose the latter one because I am looking for Kindle books that I haven't read yet.

So can you see the importance of choosing the right two categories for your Kindle book? I must also note that Amazon places your Kindle book in categories that they deem fit so don't be alarmed when this happens to you. You might end up in a category or subcategory that might seem a bit strange.

The Secret Strategy That You Can Use to Choose Your Kindle Book's Categories

So how should you go about choosing the best two categories for your Kindle book? Let me share my secret strategy of how I choose mine. The first thing I do is go to the Amazon site and in the search drop down menu I choose "Kindle store" and then I click on the "Go" button which takes me straight to the Amazon Kindle store. Then on the side panel of the web page where it says "Kindle store department" I choose Kindle ebooks.

This brings up a list of the overall categories for books in the side panel of the web page. I then look for the most appropriate overall category for my book and once I have found it I then click on that category.

Let's say for this particular example that overall general category is "Business and Investing". I would then click on "Business and Investing" and what comes up next is a list of subcategories and these particular subcategories each have the total amount of Kindle books that are listed in them.

I would then quickly scan and analyze the total amount of books in each appropriate subcategory for my Kindle book in the business investing genre with the strategic purpose of locating the most popular subcategory as well as the least popular subcategory based on the total amount of books listed.

I know that your head is probably spinning at this point, so let me clearly explain why I want to list my Kindle book in the most popular subcategory as well as in the least popular subcategory. When someone buys another book in that popular subcategory that my Kindle book is listed in chances are that my book will show up as an additional "recommended choice" which gives me more exposure and increases my chances to make a sale.

The strategic purpose of also listing my book in the least popular subcategory is the competition is less steep so my book has a greater chance of being discovered. In addition to having a greater chance of being discovered it also has a great chance of making Amazon's best sellers list in that particular subcategory.

In concluding the topic on choosing a category for your Kindle book, you must make sure that the subcategories that you decide on are listed as choices in the Amazon Kindle Direct Publishing program.

How to Market Your Kindle Book by Creating a Listmania

A great way to promote and market your Kindle book is by creating Listmanias. What are Listmanias? Listmanias are simply "lists" that you can create on Amazon. Amazon allows anyone with a registered account to create a "list" of their favorite things like for example a "list" of their favorite books.

The way that you would use a Listmania to promote your particular Kindle book is by creating a list that includes your own book with other popular books that cover the same subject or genre. For example, you can create a top ten list in your book's genre and place your book at the top of the list or near the top of the list and include the more popular books than yours below it.

The chances are if people see your book positioned right alongside a list of popular books, there is a high degree of probability that they will buy your book because it looks desirable. Plus maybe they have already purchased the other books on your top ten list and your book is the only one that they don't have in their collection.

So are you starting to see how this would work for you? I know that you are probably thinking and saying to yourself "but wouldn't I be promoting my competition?" The answer is yes. However, the main reason why you would want to include your Kindle book with your competitors is because it provides the perfect opportunity to cross promote your book with best-selling titles that are in your book's genre.

By including the best-selling titles in your list, you are able to attract a targeted audience to your Kindle book. In addition, when a search is performed on Amazon for one or more of the popular books in your list, your Listmania may appear as a recommendation below that particular book or in the side panel of the book's product page.

Another advantage of creating a Listmania is that they rank very well in Google's search engine. So you want to make sure that you've optimized your list accordingly using relevant keywords in the description, in your book's title, as well as in the title of your Listmania to maximize your exposure in the major search engines.

Getting search engine traffic to your Listmania can be a real financial bonanza for you, so don't take this task lightly. To create a Listmania for your Kindle book just do the following the steps:

1) Register with Amazon if you are not already
2) Visit your profile page and log into your account
3) Click the "Edit Your Profile" button on the top right-hand corner of the page.
4) Click the "Lists" tab in the Contributions section of Your Profile.
5) Click the "Create your first one now" link.
6) Provide the requested information for your list and click the preview button to review your list and if you are satisfied with how it looks publish it.

Before you actually publish your list here is the information that you will be asked to enter:

- Name Your List: Enter a catchy title for your list (make sure it includes your main keywords).
- Your qualifications: Your qualifications should be a description of why you're an expert in the subject of your list.
- Introduction: You can add an optional introductory paragraph to describe the list.
- Add a product: This is what makes your list. You can add anything from the product listings on Amazon.com.

Amazon's Search Engine

The great thing that I always loved about Amazon's search engine is that it is a "buyer's search engine". When people go to search for something on Amazon they usually are searching with the intentions of buying something, whereas on Google people mainly are searching for information. Since Amazon is a buyer's search engine and is a tool that people primarily use to find and buy books it is essential that your Kindle book has a high visibility on it.

The way that you position yourself to be found on Amazon's search engine is by optimization. Optimization includes having your keywords in your description and in the case of non-fiction in your book's title. It also helps a great deal when you put relevant keywords as search words in the details page when you are uploading your Kindle book in the Kindle Direct Publishing program.

Your keywords are words that are related to your book's topic, as well as the words that people would typically use in a search query when searching to find a book in your book's genre. For example, if your Kindle book was on dog training, dog training would be one of your keywords. A typical search query that people would enter in the search engine to find a book that's on dog training would be "How To Train A Dog", this is known a keyword phrase.

Optimizing your book's title, description and keywords is quite easy for non-fiction books and if you optimize well and your book sales are decent relative to the other books that are also optimized for the same main keywords, you will more than likely land on the first page of Amazon's search results.

In fact, I go over this in more detail in the section right after this one entitled How To Rank On The First Page Of Google and Amazon For Your Non-Fiction Kindle Book. You might even snare the coveted #1 position on the first page of the search results like I did for my book entitled **"How To Market Your Business Online and Offline"**. As of this writing if you do a search using in any of the following keyword phrases "how to market a business online", "how to market a business offline" you will see that my book occupies the number 1 position on Amazon.

The only real way to optimize for a fiction book is by using keywords that are typical in your Kindle book's genre. For example, if it were an erotica fiction book some of those keywords would be:

- Erotica
- Erotica Romance
- Erotica Fiction
- Erotic
- Erotica Novel
- Erotica Book

However, since these keywords are so general the only way to rank on the first page of the search results for a fiction book is if your book sells extremely well. This is so because Amazon sorts the rankings based on the amount of current sales a book has. So with fiction books the main way they are found in Amazon's search engine is by entering in the exact book title and name of the author.

The only other ways to enhance your book's visibility on Amazon's search engine is by "tagging", creating Listmanias, or So You'd Like to ....Guides. In the case of the latter two, your book will appear indirectly in Amazon's search engine by being included in a Listmania list, or a So You'd Like to Guide.

So You'd Like to... Guides

So You'd Like to...Guides are a way for you to help other customers find all the items and information they might need for something they are interested in. A So You'd Like to...Guide includes a short, informative article targeting people who are interested in your genre and is connected to your book's detail page and to other similar best-selling books.

So You'd Like to...Guides include more details and contain more information than Listmanias.

How To Rank On The First Page Of Google and Amazon For Your Non-Fiction Kindle Book

You can achieve first page rankings on Google's search engine for your Kindle book if it's non-fiction and if you've optimized your book's title as well as the description of it by including the main keywords in which you want to rank for.

For example, before actually choosing a title for this particular book I created a list of relevant keywords or keyword phrases that people would use in their search query when looking to find resources or information on how to promote a Kindle book.

The main keywords and keyword phrases I came up with were the following:

"How To Market A Kindle Book"

"How To Promote A Kindle Book"

"Kindle Book Marketing"

"How To Sell A Kindle Book"

I then used Google's keyword tool to determine whether people were actually using those particular keywords in any combination in their search queries and if so I wanted to determine what specific keywords were getting the most searches.

By the way, you can determine this by entering your keywords in the keyword tool and clicking on the submit button. When the results are rendered it will show you the amount of local searches as well as the amount of global searches that have occurred. This is based on a monthly average.

Since I reside in the United States, "local searches" for me would represent all searches that were made in Google's search engine in the United States. Global searches simply represent the number of searches that have occurred in Google's search engine outside of the United States which are basically worldwide searches.

Once I was finished with my keyword research, I was looking to come up with a book title that would not only get traction in Google's search engine but in Amazon's search engine as well. The bottom line for me was I wanted my targeted audience to simply be able to find my book easily on both Amazon's and Google's search engine.

With that goal in mind the title and subtitle I strategically settled on was "How To Promote Market And Sell Your Kindle Book: Amazon Kindle Publishing Marketing and Promotion Guide". I know that the subtitle may seem to be a bit too long but my research indicated that I would gain an advantage and get more eyeballs by putting in the long tail keyword phrase "Amazon Kindle Publishing" in the subtitle.

What most Kindle book authors don't realize is that it is far more easier to get your Kindle book's product page on Amazon to rank on the first page of Google's search engine than it is a website.

Here's why. Google views Amazon as a "trusted" website but on the other hand other lesser known websites like my own or perhaps yours have to consistently earn Google's trust to be considered as a website that has a reliable source of information.

One variable that Google uses to determine if a site is influential and therefore should rank high in their search engines is by the amount of quality backlinks a site has.

Backlinks also referred to as inbound links are links that are directed towards a website from other websites.

The more quality backlinks a website has, the more Google considers it as being an influential and authority site. This is because other websites have essentially voted for it by linking to it. In most cases, if a website is search engine optimized and has more quality backlinks than its competitors, it will more than likely outrank them and land on the first page of Google for its main keywords.

So how does all of this relate to getting your Kindle book to rank on the first page of Google? Number one if you've inserted your main keywords in the title of your book as well as in the description area of your book's product page on Amazon you are well optimized. Number two, this will ultimately result in your page being recognized and indexed by Google and other search engines.

The only thing you would have to do now is build quality backlinks to the url address of your Kindle book's product page on Amazon. That url is given to you by Amazon once your Kindle book has been approved and a product page has been created for it.

For example, in my Kindle book entitled **"Search Engine Domination"** where you can learn more on how to rank on the first page of Google the url for the product page is the following:

http://www.amazon.com/dp/B007BNZOCS

The end part of that particular url address contains the book's ASIN number. So to get the exact url of your Kindle book's product page, all you would have to do is replace my book's ASIN number with yours.

For example, the ASIN number of another book that I've authored entitled **"The Secrets Of Making $10,000 On Ebay in 30 Days"** is B008NOI1MO. To get the exact url to that book's product page I would just remove the ASIN number from the url of the previous example and replace it with the new ASIN. After I've done that it would look exactly like this:

http://www.amazon.com/dp/B008NOI1MO

The great thing about building backlinks for your product page on Amazon is that unlike a website you can build a ton of backlinks to it without the fear of being penalized by Google. Why? Because Google is not going to penalize Amazon because it is a "trusted" website with credibility.

How To Obtain Quality Backlinks to Your Kindle Book's Product Page

The fastest way to build and obtain quality backlinks to your Kindle book's product page is by utilizing the following methods:

Social Bookmarking

What is social bookmarking? Social bookmarking allows people to share bookmarks to websites that they think would be of interest to others. In short, social bookmarking websites are sites that categorize and store 'bookmarks' just like you would add a site to your favorites. Only in this case they are accessible to anyone on the internet.

Millions of people visit social bookmarking sites every day looking for recommended sites. These sites get millions of visitors and are great for generating targeted traffic to your Kindle book's product page and getting backlinks for it. Obtaining backlinks from social bookmarking sites will enable you to increase the search engine rankings for your Kindle book.

Here is a list of the top social bookmarking sites:

Reddit

(http://www.reddit.com)

StumbleUpon

(http://www.stumbleupon.com)

Delicious

(http://www.delicious.com)

Digg

(http://www.digg.com)

Fark

(http://www.fark.com)

Slashdot

(http://slashdot.org)

Blog Commenting Backlinks

Blog Commenting is the activity of posting feedback or comments in blog posts in order to get backlinks and referral traffic. The way it works is when you have written your comment you are asked to fill out a short form with your email address (it can be fictitious), your website's url (this would be the url of your product page) and your name (instead of inserting your name you would insert your main keyword).

Once this form is filled out and you have posted your comment you will receive a backlink from the blog. Doing this manually can be both time consuming and tedious, especially when you have to visit hundreds or thousands of blogs individually to post comments.

To make it easier for you I've created a "set it and forget it" software with a 2 minutes or less learning curve that will allow you to create blog commenting links on autopilot. The name of this software is Blog Commenting Robot and I offer a 7 day FREE TRIAL. You can sign up for your FREE TRIAL and start creating backlinks instantly to your Kindle book's product page.

Here is the 7 Day FREE TRIAL offer sign up link:

http://www.blogcommentingrobot.com/freetrial.html

Here are some of the features of Blog Commenting Robot:

- Commenting spinning -Blog Commenting Robot allows you to spin your blog comments. This will ensure that you don't have the same exact comment on every site.

- Keyword spinning -You can create backlinks for multiple keywords.

- Url spinning -You can create backlinks for multiple urls.

- Email spinning-You can use multiple email addresses.

- Multi-Threads-Blog Commenting Robot allows you to use up to 100 threads simultaneously. This is ideal for super fast posting.

- Reporting-When Blog Commenting Robot has finished creating your backlinks a detailed report is generated.

Once Again Here is the 7 Day FREE TRIAL offer sign up link:

http://www.blogcommentingrobot.com/freetrial.html

Profile Links

You can obtain backlinks by creating profile links at various websites. So what is a profile link? Profile means a page that contains membership details, and a profile link is the direct anchor text link on the profile page that links to your Kindle book product web page.

Profile links are great for link building because your links are the only links on the page which gives you maximum link juice from the main domain of the site.

Forum Posting

Forum postings in your Kindle book's niche is a great way to connect to potential customers and drive traffic to your book's page. You can obtain backlinks through your "signature" which allows you to include your product page's url and anchor text that contains your main keyword.

When you participate in the forum discussions by answering or posing questions your signature is viewable below your forum post.

Article Marketing

Article writing is a great way to garner attention for yourself as well as for your Kindle book by offering you the opportunity to show your expertise to your niche audience. Articles are also a great way to build backlinks for your Kindle book's product page. You would simply put the url of your Kindle book's product page in the resource area of the article to obtain a backlink.

Online Press Releases

Not only are online press releases a great way for your Kindle book to gain media exposure but they are also great for traffic, publicity, search engine visibility and getting backlinks.

YouTube

You can obtain a backink by creating and uploading a video to YouTube and including your Kindle book's product page url in the description area of the video. Not only is YouTube a great medium for marketing your Kindle book, but it also can be a source for obtaining quality backlinks.

If you want your Kindle book to rank on the first page of Google and sustain that ranking once it gets there, it is imperative that you consistently build backlinks to your Kindle book's product page.

If you are not fond of creating these backlinks yourself, you can simply outsource the task. My company GetSeoBacklinks.com (http://www.getseobacklinks.com) specializes in building backlinks and assisting clients to achieve first page Google rankings.

Ranking on The First Page of Amazon's Search Engine

Ranking on the first page on Amazon for a non-fiction book involves a slightly different process than getting your Kindle book's product web page to rank on the first page of Google. Google's search rankings are driven primarily by how well your book's web page is optimized for your main keywords and how many backlinks you have pointing towards it.

Whereas on Amazon backlinks are not a ranking factor and are totally irrelevant. However, what are relevant factors and will determine where you will rank on Amazon includes how well your Kindle book's title and description are optimized with your main keywords and your book sales.

Although I don't profess to know the exact algorithm that Amazon uses to determine rankings I have astutely observed, studied and analyzed the fluctuations in rankings of non-fiction Kindle books in various niches to come up with a reasonable conclusion.

To prove this is not junk theory let me give an example. I've authored two real estate investing Kindle books (they are also available in print and audio) entitled **"Creative Real Estate Investing Strategies And Tips"** and **The Creative Real Estate Marketing Equation: Motivated Sellers + Motivated Buyers =$.**

I included the keywords creative, real estate, and investing in the book's title for the first real estate book because I wanted to rank on the first page of Amazon's search engine for the keyword phrase "creative real estate investing" because I knew that was what my target audience would be primarily entering as a search query on Amazon.

For the second aforementioned real estate book I also wanted to rank on the first page of Amazon's search engine for the keyword phrase "creative real estate investing" so I included the keywords creative and real estate in the book's title and made sure I had also included the keyword "investing" in the description area.

In addition, I also included those keywords as search keywords when entering my book's details in the upload section of the Kindle Direct Publishing program. Just in case you didn't know search keywords are search terms that cause your book to appear in the search results on Amazon.

You can enter up to seven descriptive keywords, separated by commas, to help readers find your book when they search the

Kindle store. Having precise search words help target your book to readers looking for that content.

What also helps is choosing the appropriate category and subcategory. For the two real estate books the category that I chose was "real estate" and the sub category I chose was entrepreneurship.

If you do a search in Amazon's Kindle store using the search term "creative real estate investing", my two real estate investing books occupy the top two positions on the first page of the search results.

And if you did a search on the overall Amazon search engine for the search term "creative real estate investing" my book entitled "Creative Real Estate Investing Strategies And Tips" solidly occupies the number one position on the first page while my book entitled The Creative Real Estate Marketing Equation" rankings fluctuates anywhere between the number 2 position to the number 6 position at any given time.

How To Sell More Kindle Books By Creating A Series

You can sell more Kindle books by simply creating a series. However, this marketing tactic and additional income stream is often overlooked and ignored by many Kindle book authors and publishers.

The main advantages of creating a series are:

- It is an easy way to build an audience that will buy over and over again.
- Each individual book will drive the sales of the other books in the series.
- It enables you to build a loyal "tribe".
- You can grow your Kindle book sales exponentially.
- You will make more money.

Most super successful Kindle book authors like Amanda Hocking and John Locke have made a fortune by offering their books in a series format. Amanda Hocking became an instant millionaire by selling over 500,000 books of her "Trylle Trilogy" series. John Locke is infamous for his "Donovan Creed" series.

As for myself and my publishing company Make Profits Easy, we have put out books in a series format in the erotica genre by author Mack Collins. There is Seducing The Good Cop (Part 1), Seducing The Good Cop (Part 2), and Seducing The Good Cop (Part 3). There is also Toxic Seductress (Part 1) and Toxic Seductress (Part 2), Addicted To My Sugar Daddy Part 1 and Addicted To My Sugar Daddy Part 2.

In addition as I write this, author Mack Collins is working on a follow up to the book Unscrupulous Desires [Dangerous Family Secrets].

The bottom line is, books in a series format have the potential of doing really well for you because of the pre-sold audience. Speaking of selling, the clever way to sell Kindle books in a series format is by letting the readers simply know that there are other books in the series. The way that I do this is by linking each and every book with one another. I usually do this at the beginning or at the end of each book.

Creating Kindle books in a series format is not just relegated to fiction. You can also create a series with non-fiction topics. For example, "how to" type topics work especially well and are a popular genre in the Kindle book store.

Other potential examples for creating a series are recipe books. You could start with a niche recipe book that caters to a specific niche, such as gluten free dieters, low-carb dieters, raw foodist, vegans, vegetarians, diabetics, people who need to avoid certain foods because of food allergies, and so on. As an alternative, you could focus on certain cuisines or ingredients.

No matter which way that you decide to do it, once you have written and created the first book, you can simply add more recipes, and write a second, third, fourth, and fifth book. There are no limits. Are you starting to see the potential of this?

To get you started in the right direction here are some tips and strategies that will help you create your Kindle book series:

1) **Break your huge Kindle Book up into separate books** – If your Kindle book is huge you can break it up into several parts or make more than one book out of it. For example, let's say that you have ten chapters in

one book you can divide it in half to make it two books in a series. So there would be 5 chapters in book number 1 of the series and 5 chapters in book number 2 of the series.

2) **You can create niche versions of the same book** – For example, let's say that you have created a Kindle book entitled "How To Increase Sales". You can write a general book, and then you can spin the content to make it the perfect book for real estate agents, insurance brokers, car sellers, coaches, multi-level marketers, financial advisors, and so on.

All you would have to do is take the content you have already created, make some little tweaks and adjustments in the wording, add examples specific to your new target market, and Voila! You've got a new book that will attract an entirely new audience.

3) **Expound on a subtopic from the original book** – You can take a subtopic that you briefly covered in your first book and expound on it. This may require additional research but it will result in the creation of a new book in a series and the great thing about that is you already have a built in audience that is ready to make a purchase.

4) **If you have a book that has a contrasting subject or book title make it into two or more books–** What do I mean by a contrasting subject or book title? The perfect example to illustrate my point is the infamous book by John Gray entitled "Men Are from Mars, Women Are from Venus: A Practical Guide for Improving Communication and Getting What You

Want in Your Relationships".

Instead of this being just one book, to create a Kindle book series I would have made it into two books. I would have called the first book in the series "Men Are from Mars: A Woman's Practical Guide To Understanding Men and Getting What You Want in Your Relationship and I would have called the second book in the series Women Are from Venus: A Man's Practical Guide To Understanding Women and Getting What You Want in Your Relationship. You think it would have worked? Probably so and would have probably made a lot more money. Case in point, just look at the Rich Dad series by Robert Kiyosaki. It includes the best-selling book Rich Dad Poor Dad, Rich Kid Smart Kid, Cash Flow Quadrant, Rich Woman by his wife Kim and many other titles.

Another important lesson that you can learn and utilize from Robert Kiyosaki Rich Dad series is that some of the books in the series are written by other people, which goes to show you that you can also use the principle of leverage to create your Kindle book series. What type of leverage? I call it OPT which stands for other people's talent.

In conclusion of this particular topic, let me share a little secret that I use to sell my Kindle books that are in a series. The first thing I do is create all the books contained in the series. For instance, if it were a three part book series that would include part 1, part 2 and part 3.

I would then price the first book in the series to make it an impulse buy. That price is usually at.99 cents. People don't have any qualms about spending .99 cents, so if they see a

Kindle book that they are interested in offered at that price they will normally buy it even if they never heard of the author or the book. It is essentially a "no risk" purchase for them.

However, I would price part 2 and part 3 of the book series at a higher price let's say at $2.99 or higher. My reasoning for pricing the subsequent books at a higher price is of course to make more money than I did on the first book but also in my estimation the customers who bought the first book at .99 cents and had a chance to experience the quality content and value of that book shouldn't have a problem spending just a little bit more to read the second and third books in the series.

How To Scale Your Kindle Book
and Make More Money

You can make more money from your Kindle book by simply converting it to another format. This should be obvious to most Kindle book publishers but it's not and the reason why it's not is because the majority of them are thinking in a linear fashion. Linear thinking is simply thinking in the conventional way or in a straight line.

For example, most people who publish Kindle books think about the process the following way: "I will write my Kindle book, then upload it to Amazon's platform and sell it, once I sell it I will receive a royalty payment from Amazon and that's it".

Someone who thinks in a non-linear fashion or non-conventional way will go in a zig zag direction rather than a straight line. They will more than likely view the process much differently for example:

"I will write my Kindle book or get someone else to write it, after the writing is done I am going to make an audio recording of it so that I can produce an audio book, audio CD, and mp3 download and upload all three audio formats up to Amazon.

Then I am going to upload my Kindle book to the Amazon Kindle Direct Publishing program. After that upload is done, I am going to wait until Amazon approves my Kindle book's submission and it is visible in the Kindle book store. When it is visible in the Kindle book store I am then going to turn my Kindle book into a print book and publish it through the Amazon's CreateSpace print on demand platform.

Once I sell my book I will receive several royalty payments from Amazon. I will receive a royalty payment from the sales of the audio book, audio CD, mp3 download, Kindle book, and print book. I am going to make even more money from translating my printed book as well as my Kindle book into different languages or I am just going to opt to sell the foreign rights to interested parties."

I know that you probably already figured out by now that I am a non-linear thinker. If there's more money to be made by converting my Kindle book into other book formats then why not? I'm not into leaving money on the table and neither should you be especially if you want to make this a thriving business.

Having said that, let's discuss in more detail the Amazon platforms that exist that will seamlessly allow you to make available your book to the Amazon marketplace in different formats.

CreateSpace

CreateSpace is an Amazon company that has a manufacture on demand model that will enable you to sell books, videos, CDs (only music), and Amazon MP3's (only music). Manufacture on demand basically means that the printed version of your book will only be produced when a customer has ordered.

The great thing about this is there are no upfront costs for you because no investment in inventory is required. In addition, CreateSpace takes care of the customer service and order fulfillment. There are certain requirements that you must meet to turn your Kindle book into a printed book on CreateSpace. Let's go over those requirements.

Setting up your document

Select trim size. The first thing that you must do is select a trim size for your printed book. In terms of black and white books there are 15 different sizes that you can choose from. You can even choose a custom trim size however, if you choose that option your book can be sold on Amazon.com and your own eStore, but is not eligible for the bookstores and online Retailers channel within Expanded Distribution.

Speaking of distribution options, there are two options in which to choose from. There is Expanded Distribution and Standard Distribution and we will go over those two forms of distribution in detail a little bit later. Let's get back to the selection of your trim size. For black and white books here are some examples of the industry standard sizes that you can choose from:

5 inches by 8 inches

5.06 inches by 7.81 inches

5.25 inches by 8 inches

5.5 inches by 8.5 inches

6 inches by 9 inches

There are 12 industry standard sizes with black and white books. For color books there are 7 industry standard sizes. There are also submission requirements in regards to the size of margins and page count. These requirements are listed on the CreateSpace website at www.createspace.com. To make it easier for you CreateSpace offers Word document templates that matches the trim size you want for your book.

The page size and margins are automatically set for each template so you don't have to concern yourself with trying to figure that out. Once you have entered and formatted your book's content in the Word provided template and you are satisfied how it looks, you have to convert your Word document to a PDF file to upload it to CreateSpace.

Creating your book cover. To create your book cover CreateSpace once again provides you with PDF cover templates that you can use to create your cover. You more than likely want to use the same front cover that you used for your Kindle book and you can, all you would have to do is format it to fit into the PDF provided cover template and create a back cover and a spine for it.

Once you have completed your cover you are now ready to upload it along with your book to the CreateSpace website, but before uploading your book and its cover CreateSpace will prompt you to enter in your book details. Your book details include such information as the title of your book, author's name, the publication date etc.

When you have completed entering in your book details you then have to choose your ISBN option. An ISBN, or International Standard Book Number, is a unique 10- or 13-digit number assigned to every published book and it is printed on the back cover. An ISBN identifies a title's edition, publisher, and physical properties such as trim size, page count, and binding type.

You are given four ISBN options in which to choose from and the ISBN option that you choose will determine if you or CreateSpace will be listed as the imprint or distributor.

The 4 ISBN options:

1) **Free CreateSpace-Assigned ISBN** - CreateSpace will assign an ISBN to your book free of charge. They will be listed as the imprint of record.

2) **Custom ISBN** - A Custom ISBN will allow your own imprint to be listed as the publisher. The cost for a Custom ISBN is $10 and it will allow you to sell on Amazon's United States and European websites, the CreateSpace eStore and in some Expanded distribution channels. The Expanded Distribution channels that your book won't be eligible to be distributed to are Libraries and Academic Institutions outlet.

3) **Custom Universal ISBN**-- A Custom Universal ISBN will allow your own imprint to be listed as the publisher and you can use this particular ISBN with any publisher whereas with the Free CreateSpace Assigned ISBN and the Custom ISBN can only be used with the CreateSpace Independent Publishing Platform.

   The cost for a Custom Universal ISBN is $99 and it will allow you to sell on Amazon's United States and European websites, the CreateSpace eStore and in some Expanded distribution channels. The Expanded Distribution channels that your book won't be eligible to be distributed to are Libraries and Academic Institutions outlet.

4) **Provide Your Own ISBN** – You can provide your own ISBN to CreateSpace. You can purchase your own ISBN from a company called Bowker or through a local ISBN agency. If you are providing your own ISBN, your

book's imprint must match what's on file with your ISBN.

Uploading and Reviewing Your Book

You are now ready to upload your book and its cover to the CreateSpace website for processing. This is a very simple, easy and quick process. Once your book is finished uploading you can check the interior to see how it looks using the Interior Reviewer before submitting it for final processing. If you are satisfied with the way your book looks, you can click on the submit button and it will be reviewed by CreateSpace. The review process usually takes 24-48 hours.

If your book passes the review you will get an email stating that your submission is waiting for your final approval. You can review your entire book including how the cover looks digitally or you can choose to order a physical copy of your book to be sent to you for review.

If everything looks fine, all you have to do next is approve it. Once you have approved it, you have to set up your distribution channels and pricing.

Distribution Channels

Once you are member of CreateSpace (it's free) your book is instantly eligible for **Standard Distribution**. With **Standard Distribution** you can sell your book on Amazon.com, Amazon Europe which presently includes Amazon.co.uk (United Kingdom), Amazon.de (Germany), Amazon.es (Spain), Amazon.fr (France), and Amazon.it (Italy).

With Standard Distribution you can also sell your book in your own eStore that CreateSpace gives to you. You are allowed to customize your eStore to match your website and CreateSpace handles the fulfillment of all your orders.

Standard Distribution also includes making your book available through the Kindle Direct Publishing program. In fact, if you already have a Kindle book uploaded to the Kindle Publishing program it will automatically be linked to your printed version of your book giving your customers the chance to choose between either version.

Expanded Distribution – Expanded distribution cost $25 and offers you the opportunity to access a larger audience via online retailers, bookstores, libraries, academic institutions, and distributors within the United States.

Setting The Price of Your Printed Book

The amount of royalties that you will make from each book sold is based on the price that you set it at, the trim size of the book, the interior type (black and white or color book) and the amount of pages that it contains. To figure out the royalty you will make for each book sold CreateSpace has a royalty calculator on its site. The royalty calculator calculates how much money you will make from each distribution channel.

In fact, this is the first thing that you should determine before choosing your book's trim size, because the trim size that you choose will affect the amount of pages your book contains and these variables will determine the manufacturing costs of your book which is automatically deducted from your royalty payment for each book sold.

Calculating The Royalties From Your Printed Book

For example, using the royalty calculator to determine how much I will earn from each book sold that has a list price of $11.99, a trim size of 5.25 inches by 8 inches, a black and white interior and contains 200 pages I come up with the following royalty amounts for each distribution channel.

- **Amazon.com** = $3.94
- **eStore** = $6.34
- **Expanded Distribution** = $1.54
- **Amazon Europe** (for books printed in Great Britain) = £1.74
- **Amazon Europe** (for books printed in Continental Europe) = €2.44

In this new example, I'm going to use the same variables as the last example with the exception of the amount pages and the trim size. I will change the amount of pages to 300 and change the trim size to 6"inches by 9 inches. Here are the results for the royalty amounts for each distribution channel.

- **Amazon.com** = $2.74
- **eStore** = $5.14
- **Expanded Distribution** = $.34
- **Amazon Europe** (for books printed in Great Britain) = £1.74
- **Amazon Europe** (for books printed in Continental Europe) = €1.24

In this particular example you may want to pass on paying $25 for the Expanded Distribution because the royalty rate is a bit low at .34 cents unless of course you think that you will be selling a great deal of books using Expanded Distribution.

Obviously, your printed book will be priced higher than your Kindle book because one is delivered digitally and doesn't incur any manufacturing or delivery cost (with the exception of the small delivery fee that Amazon charges to deliver your Kindle book electronically) and the other one incurs a cost to manufacture. In the case of the printed book the delivery or shipping costs are passed on to the customer.

Royalty Payments

To receive royalty payments from CreateSpace you must enter in your royalty payment information in your royalty profile located in the account settings. You can elect to either be paid by check or through direct deposit. If you choose to be paid by check you will be issued a royalty payment once your royalty earnings exceed $100 and there is an $8 handling fee to process checks.

If you elect to be paid via direct deposit there is no handling fee and you will be paid once your royalty earnings reach $10. Unlike in the Kindle Direct Publishing program there isn't any 60 day initial waiting period before you get paid. For example, if you've earned royalties in December and you meet the payment threshold, you will receive your royalty payment 30 days later which is in the month of January.

You are almost ready to launch your printed book into the Amazon ecosystem. The only things that are left for you to do is enter a description of your book, (it should match the description of your Kindle book so that they will automatically be linked together), the BISAC category information, the title of your book, (if you haven't entered it already) your search keywords and the price of your book.

Once you have completed this, you are finally ready to officially make your book available to the public. To make this happen all you would have to do is hit the final approve button and your book will become available.

ACX (Audiobook Creation Exchange)

ACX short for Audiobook Creation Exchange is an Amazon company that is part of Audible and Audible is a subsidiary of Amazon. ACX essentially is a marketplace where professional authors, agents, publishers, and other Rights Holders can post fallow audio book rights. It will allow you to scale your Kindle book by converting it into an audio book which puts you in the position to realize additional revenue streams.

Surprisingly, not too many Kindle book authors or publishers are exploiting this option and I don't understand their logic. Maybe it's because they simply don't know about it or know about it but think that it involves a complex process where they have do the recording of the audio book themselves , which is so far from the actual truth.

The fact of the matter is that through ACX you can have someone else record the audio for your Kindle book if you are the rights holder of the book. You can search for potential narrators by searching through the ACX database or narrators, audio book studios, and other producers will find your book on the ACX website located at www.acx.com and proactively audition to record your book.

In addition, an audio publisher searching ACX can message you about buying the audio rights directly from you and finally you can even choose to record the audio book yourself.

For your audio book to be eligible for upload to ACX you must be a resident of the United States, have a US mailing address, a valid US Taxpayer Identification Number (TIN), and you have to submit a W9 form.

How to Make an Offer for the Production of Your Audio Book

There are two ways that you can make an offer to a producer for the production of your audio book. You have to decide which option is best for you before making your offer.

The two ways are:

1) Pay For Production Deal

2) Royalty Share Deal

A **Pay For Production Deal** is a binding agreement where you agree to pay the producer or narrator a flat-fee per finished hour of your book.

A **Royalty Share Deal** is a binding agreement where you agree to a 50-50 split of the royalties with the producer for the production of the audio book.

If you want to keep your royalty revenue for yourself and you don't want to pay anyone any type of fees to produce your audio book, I suggest that you do it yourself. It is really much easier than you think. You don't have to go out and purchase some elaborate studio equipment either.

There is a free virtual recording and editing tool available called Audacity that will enable you to produce a quality recording of your book right on your computer. The only piece of equipment you would have to purchase is a condensed USB microphone that has bi-directional headphone monitoring and management built into its base and a pair of headphones if you don't have any already. The condensed microphone that works the best with Audacity is the Samson G Track USB microphone. You can purchase this microphone on Ebay for $80 -$100.

Distribution Options For Your Audio Book

Your audio book that you upload to ACX will be distributed to:

Audible.com

Amazon.com

iTunes

Audible.com, Amazon.com and iTunes are leading digital retailers that reach the vast majority of audio book buyers. You can sell your audio book elsewhere to other retailers however if you decide to do that on your own or through another entity you have to sign a non-exclusive agreement with ACX and as a result of choosing this option your royalty pay-out from their distribution will be much less.

There are two types of agreements in which to choose from when selling your audio book via ACX. There is the exclusive agreement and the non-exclusive agreement. With the exclusive agreement you can only sell your audio book through ACX distribution channels which includes Audible.com, Amazon.com and iTunes.

You can not sell your audio book anywhere else and that includes your own website. If you opt for the exclusive agreement your royalty pay-out will be 50% of the listed price of your audio book which ACX sets.

The non-exclusive agreement enables you to sell your audio book through the ACX distribution channels (Audible.com,

Amazon.com and ITunes) as well as anywhere else but your royalty pay-out will be 25% of each unit sold by and through ACX.

Regardless of what agreement you choose each agreement stipulates that ACX has the right to distribute your audio book for seven years.

You have to thoroughly and carefully consider your options before signing an agreement with ACX, because you are entering in a legal binding agreement and by law you must honor the terms.

The type of agreement you enter in whether it is a non-exclusive agreement or an exclusive agreement should be determined by your overall strategy. For instance, maybe you don't have a problem signing an exclusive agreement because you are satisfied with only selling your audio book through ACX's distribution channels and you could less about selling through other retailers. If that's your strategy then an exclusive agreement will work perfectly for you.

However, on the contrary maybe you do want to sell your audio book through other retailers, your own website, as well as through ACX. If that is your case, then a non-exclusive agreement will work perfectly for this type of situation.

Perhaps you may even decide to scale your audio book even further by turning it into a Audio book CD, Audio book CD set or even a MP3 download and you want to sell through the Amazon Marketplace, your own website as well as other distribution outlets while also being able to sell your audio book through ACX's distribution channel then once again a non-exclusive agreement would be your best option.

Personally, since I have different revenue strategies for each audio book that I have, the type of agreement that I enter into will vary. For example, for this particular book I chose the exclusive agreement because I don't have any plans to sell it through any other distribution outlets. However, for my book entitled "How To Market Your Business Online and Offline" the scenario is quite different as I plan to distribute both the Audio book CD and mp3 version of the book to other retail outlets including the Amazon Marketplace.

Please understand that this is not meant as legal advice, you should do your own due diligence by thoroughly reviewing each and every binding agreement that you enter in with ACX. The agreements are very easy to understand, but if you are having trouble understanding them you should call ACX directly or consult with an attorney.

Whispersync for Voice and Immersion Reading

Whispersync for voice is a breakthrough technology that allows you to switch back and forth between reading a Kindle book and listening to the companion Audible audio book without losing your space. For example, say if you've listened half-way through chapter 5 of an audio book while in your car but instead of listening you have the urge to read more of the book once you got home, your Kindle will bring you in the text exactly to where you stopped listening.

Whispersync for immersion reading allows readers to synchronize Kindle text with the Audible audio version of the book. Also while they are reading, the text in the ebook is highlighted as the audio track moves along, making it easier for the reader to follow along.

ACX offers your audio book the opportunity to be made available for sale as a companion to the Kindle book for customers who want to make use of the Whispersync and Immersion Reading features of the Kindle. However, to be eligible your audio book must meet certain requirements. One of those requirements is your audio book must match the text of the Kindle book version of it. ACX rules also require that your audio book has a 97% sync rate.

As you can clearly see there are many financial benefits that you can possible gain by creating an audio version of your book that is whole concept behind "scaling".

Audio Book Pricing

The retailers that make up the ACX's distribution channels independently prices your Audio book and determines such price at their sole discretion. This is the only drawback that I see with the ACX program, the inability to set your own price for your audio book. In the case of Audible.com the price of your audio book is determined according to the length of the recording. Here is a break-down of how Audible determines pricing.

Under 3 hours: under $10

3 – 5 hours: $10 - $20

5–10 hours: $15 - $25

10–20 hours: $20 - $30

Over 20 hours: $25 - $35

Audio Book Royalties

In regards to royalties, ACX uses an escalator royalty system and you can earn up to 90% depending on the options you choose and the sales of your digital audio book. For example, if you chose exclusive distribution your royalty rate starts off at 50% of the retail price and escalates 1% each time you reach a certain sales threshold. So you basically will start off at a 50% royalty rate and have the ability to move it all the way up to a 90% royalty based on your total amount of sales.

If you chose to record your own audio book or you chose the pay per production deal with a producer, for every 500 sales your royalty rate increases by 1 %. Here's a brief example.

From 0 to 500 Units-50.0%

From 501 to 1000 Units -51.0%

From 1001 to 1500 Units-52.0%

From 1501 to 2000 Units-53.0%

From 2001 to 2500 Units-54.0%

As you can clearly see under the exclusive distribution where you either recording your own audio book or paid a flat fee for it to be produced, the royalty escalates by 1% for each 500 sales until it reaches the max of a 90% royalty rate. To receive a 90% royalty rate under the exclusive distribution agreement you would have to sell 20,010 units.

Under a royalty share exclusive distribution agreement the numbers are basically the same except you will splitting the royalties 50/50 with the producer that you entered in the royalty share agreement with. For example, if you sold 500 audio books you are at the 50% royalty rate however 25% of this would have to be shared with the producer of the audio book.

Under the non-exclusive distribution agreement, your royalty rate will start off at 25% and also escalate 1% for every 500 units sold however the maximum it will escalate to is 70%. Here is a brief example.

From 0 to 500 Units-25.0%

From 501 to 1000 Units -26.0%

From 1001 to 1500 Units-27.0%

From 1501 to 2000 Units-28.0%

From 2001 to 2500 Units-29.0%

You will receive your royalty payments every month from ACX if your audio book has made at least $50 in sales. In concluding this topic, I hope I have clearly shown you how ACX represents a golden opportunity for you to add an additional revenue stream by simply converting your Kindle book to an audio book.

How To Sell Your Audio Book CD on Amazon

Sellers on Amazon Marketplace are allowed to sell a variety of products however for our purposes we are only interested in converting and selling our Kindle book as an audio book CD or audio book CD set because many people still listen to CDs and we want to be able to offer that segment of the marketplace that choice plus that's an additional revenue stream for us.

I rarely ever see this strategy being used because it's kind of difficult for people to think "outside of the Kindle book box" simply because selling Kindle books is the latest craze and rightly so because it spawned a new, revolutionary and cool way to sell books to the masses. Although we appreciate that fact as self publishers, we are not trying to get caught up in the Kindle book hysteria to the point where we are leaving out potential revenue streams.

It's really quite easy to create an audio book CD. As mentioned earlier all you would have to do is use a free recording and editing tool like Audacity, have a compatible Samson G Track USB condensed microphone, and a basic pair of headphones and you are off to the races.

Print on Demand CDs

Once you have made your recording the next thing you would have to do is choose a print on demand fulfillment CD service. You want to choose a print on demand fulfillment service because you don't want to go out and invest in a bunch of inventory and you don't want any upfront costs. You basically just want to order your audio book CDs when you get actual customer orders or when you choose to participate in Amazon

Advantage fulfillment program where they require for you to
have a certain amount of inventory in stock to fulfill your
orders.

Kunaki located at www.kunaki.com is a great print on demand
digital manufacturing service that you can use that has no
order minimums. The way that the process works with Kunaki
is you design and configure your product (case, disc, inserts,
cover art, contents) with their publishing software.

The software renders a precise 3-D replica of your product and
lets you modify and review different possibilities. The software
compiles your product's content, packaging, art-work into a
single digital file and uploads it to their facility.

When you are ready to order, you just enter your customer's
information and make your payment, and Kunaki
manufactures your audio book CD and ships your customer a
full-color, glossy, fully assembled, cellophane-wrapped, high-
quality, retail-ready CD that contains a free UPC bar code.

The cost to order CDs at Kunaki is $1.00 per unit when you
order 5 or less CDs and included in this price are:

- Manufacturing
- Assembly
- Full color CD printing
- Jewel case
- Full color 2-panel insert
- Full color tray card
- Cellophane wrapping
- UPC bar code
- 24 hour manufacturing

When you order 6 or more units the price is $1.75 per unit and both prices quoted does not include the shipping costs that are involved.

Now that you know how to create and manufacture your audio book CD let's discuss how to sell it on Amazon.

The Amazon Marketplace and Amazon.com Advantage

There are two ways that you can list your audio book CD on Amazon:

1) Amazon.com Advantage

2) Amazon Marketplace

Advantage is a self-service consignment program that enables you to promote your audio book CD directly on Amazon.com. The way that it works is you have to first join Advantage and the cost of doing so is $29.95 for a 1 year membership. Once you are a member you would add your audio book CD title to your Advantage account.

Amazon would then order a conservative quantity of them and their goal for doing this is they want to make sure that they have enough quantity to meet current demand as well as possible future orders in the weeks ahead.

Once your inventory is received by Amazon it is stored in one of their fulfillment centers and it will be available for purchase on Amazon. When your audio book CD is purchased on Amazon's site they will ship those orders out for you.

I must note that in order to sell your audio book CD on Amazon it must contain a scannable ISBN, UPC, or EAN bar code and be cellophane wrapped. That's why I strongly suggest that you use Kunaki as your print on demand CD service because not only do they provide you with a free scannable UPC bar code, your audio book CD is cellophane wrapped and they will also manufacture and drop-ship your audio book CDs to Amazon and restock them when needed.

How and When You Get Paid by The Amazon Advantage Program

If you chose to sell your audio book CD through Amazon's Advantage program you will earn 45% of the listed price of your item and Amazon gets the remaining 55%. So if you were selling your audio book CD for $17.99 you will earn $8.10 for each unit sold and Amazon will receive $9.89

You will receive payment for your audio book CDs sold through the Advantage program automatically at the end of the month following the month in which your product is sold. For example, for items sold in the month of January, they will pay you at the end of February. Payment can be made to you by Electronic Funds Transfer (EFT) to a U.S. bank account or by paper check.

If you opt to receive payment via paper check, your payment will not be disbursed until you reach a threshold of $100 and there is a $15 processing fee per check.

Amazon Marketplace

You can list your audio book CD through Amazon's Marketplace but it requires a Pro Merchant Subscription to do so. The cost of a Pro Merchant subscription is $39.99 per month. Whatever you do (unless you already have a Pro Merchant subscription on Amazon because you are selling other products) do not pay the $39.99 per month fee to have your audio book CD listed in the Amazon marketplace.

Here's what you do instead. Amazon offers a 30 day free trial for a Pro Merchant Subscription and you should use it to list your audio book CD for free. The way that you would list your audio book CD is via your Seller Central account. Seller Central is the Web interface used to manage all aspects of selling on Amazon.com. There you can add product information, make inventory updates, manage orders, and manage payments though a suite of Web-based and downloadable tools.

A smart way to list your inventory without never having to update the quantity again is by entering in a high number where it ask you how many units that you have in stock. The number that I normally put is 5,000 units that way I don't have to worry about it for a while.

How and When You Get Paid As a Seller in Amazon's Marketplace

As a seller in Amazon's marketplace you are responsible for shipping out your own audio book CDs for customers who have ordered it. The great thing about that is Amazon collects from the customer the shipping cost which you can then apply when you ship the item. That is one of the main differences between selling via the Amazon Marketplace and selling via the Advantage program.

Another huge difference is the amount of money you make from each unit sold. As a seller in the Amazon Marketplace you earn about 85% of the total list price for each unit sold. Amazon makes about a 15% commission. I'd rather make 85% over the 55% that the Advantage program pays so as I result I ship out my own audio book CDs for now.

In addition, when you sell via the Advantage program Amazon doesn't share your customer's information with you like their name and address. On the other hand as a seller in Amazon's Marketplace those details are shared with you which allows you to build and cultivate a customer list.

You get paid from Amazon services when they have "settled" your account. This occurs every 14 days. Whenever your account has been settled and you have a positive balance from your sales Amazon transfers your funds to your bank account using an Automated Clearing House (ACH) or electronic funds transfer.

How To Sell The Translation and Foreign Rights To Your Kindle Book

Selling the translations rights to your Kindle book or selling the foreign rights to it will enable you to realize additional income. In addition to more income there are several other advantages as well, like gaining more readers and exposing your book to a global audience. Unfortunately most Kindle book authors have never even considered selling the translation or foreign rights to their book and so it remains an untapped gold mine.

Either they are not familiar with the concept of selling translation or foreign rights to their book or they are aware of it but they think that the process involved is complicated. So what is the concept behind selling translation or foreign rights? In a nutshell this is when you give foreign publishers the right to translate your book into different languages and sell it and as a result you will receive an advance plus royalty payments from it. However, in most cases involving foreign publishers, after you have received an advance that is usually the last payment that you will receive.

If you decide to use a literary agent this is how the process usually goes:

1) First you have to decide whether or not your book is worthy of being translated, has universal appeal or has foreign rights potential.

2) Then you have to locate literary agents or people who specialize in selling foreign rights.

3) The literary agent after signing an agreement with you (which stipulates that they will a get 15% to 20% commission for selling your foreign rights) then takes your book and promotes it to the various foreign entities. This is an expense to you and you either have to give the literary agent copies of your book or you have to send them out yourself. To save money, try sending out your book to the various interested parties electronically.

4) You enter in an agreement with the foreign publisher or multiple foreign publishers and you are paid an advance from each for doing so. The deal terms are usually structured from 3-7 years and grants the right to the foreign entity to translate, publish, manufacture and sell your book in the language agreed upon.

   The foreign publishers translate your book at their own expense, so you don't have to worry about that because it should be included in the agreement. Other things that you should make sure that is spelled out in the agreement:

   - Definition of the specific language and territory that your book will be sold in.
   - The format that it will be published and sold as. For example: paperback, hardcover, or audio book.
   - Design and creative control.
   - Dates for the accounting of sales and royalties.

The advances that you receive from each foreign publisher will vary but collectively added up you can make thousands upon thousands of dollars.

Ok now that you know how lucrative selling the translation or foreign rights to your Kindle book can be, it's time for you to make a connection with literary and foreign right agents that are experienced and can assist you. To help you in this matter, I have conveniently compiled a list of 850 plus literary and foreign rights agents. This list can be obtained at:

http://www.makeprofitsnow.com/agents.html

Conclusion

Whew – we sure covered a ton of cutting edge ideas, didn't we? Hopefully you have a clear understanding of each and every idea, concept and strategy that was presented in this book and you are totally revved up to begin implementing them.

As you can see, this is all stuff that most people are perfectly capable of doing. It doesn't involve any difficult skill and in no time you will be able to master it all. However, you must always remember that your success lies in the execution of the strategies.

What is execution? Execution is about taking those strategies mentioned and making sure they are implemented with power. The bottom line is any strategy without execution is hallucination. If you don't execute all you really have are idle ideas that lack kinetic energy.

I hope this book has been extremely helpful to you in your efforts to effectively promote, market and sell your Kindle book. If you have found the information to be of value and you think that it can help others with their journey as Kindle book publishers, I would highly appreciate it if you took the time out to share it on Facebook, Twitter, Google+ etc.

I wish you the best of luck with all of your publishing efforts and let's have a toast in honor of your next bestselling Kindle book. It's waiting for you to write it and tell the world about it.

Thanks and much success,

Omar Johnson

Other Books By Author

How To Create A Profitable Ezine From Scratch

The Secrets Of Making $10,000 on Ebay in 30 Days

The Complete Guide To Investing in Gold And Silver: Surviving The Great Economic Depression

How To Sell Any Product Online:"Secrets of The Killer Sales Letter"

How To Make A Fortune Using The Public Domain

Search Engine Domination: The Ultimate Secrets To Increasing Your Website's Visibility And Making A Ton Of Cash

Creative Real Estate Investing Strategies And Tips

How to Make Money Online:"The Savvy Entrepreneur's Guide To Financial Freedom"

How to Overcome Your Self-Limiting Beliefs & Achieve Anything You Want

The Secrets of Finding The Perfect Ghostwriter For Your Book

The Creative Real Estate Marketing Equation: Motivated Sellers + Motivated Buyers = $

How To Start An Online Business With Less Than $200

How To Market Your Business Online and Offline

www.ingramcontent.com/pod-product-compliance
Lightning Source LLC
Chambersburg PA
CBHW051525170526
45165CB00002B/605